SHARKS
& UNDERWATER MONSTERS

SHARKS
& UNDERWATER MONSTERS

PAULA HAMMOND

📖 SCHOLASTIC

www.scholastic.com

This edition published by Scholastic Inc., 557 Broadway, New York, NY 10012 by arrangement with Amber Books Ltd.

Scholastic Canada Ltd.
Markham, Ontario

1 2 3 4 5 6 7 8 9 10

ISBN: 978-0-545-36627-4

Editorial and design by
Amber Books Ltd
Bradley's Close
74–77 White Lion Street
London N1 9PF
United Kingdom
www.amberbooks.co.uk

Project Editor: Sarah Uttridge
Design: Keren Harragan

Printed in Shenzhen, China

Picture credits:

Illustrations: International Book Management, www.ibm.gb.com © Amber Books Ltd

Maps: Patrick Mulrey

Photographs:
Alamy: 46 (Wolfgang Polzer)
Bigstock: 12 (Michael Madelung), 82 (Dmitry Rukhlenko)
Corbis: 8 (Jeffrey L. Rotman), 14 (Ralph Clevenger), 18 (Richard Herrmann), 28 (Lawson Wood), 38 (Visuals Unlimited), 48 (Brandon D. Cole), 52 (Norbert Wu), 74 (David Wrobel)
Dreamstime: 10 (Carol Buchanan), 24 (Krzysztof Odziomek), 26 (Katseyephoto), 32 (Stephan Kerhofs), 60 (Dean Bertoncelj), 72 (Ricardo Bazarin), 84 (John Anderson), 92 (Melvin Lee), 94 (Luizrocha)
FLPA: 16 (Reinhard Dirscherl), 20 (Richard Herrmann), 34 (Photo Researchers), 36 (Fred Bavendam), 42 (Brigitte Wilms), 44 (Norbert Wu), 56 (Norbert Probst), 62 (Michael Durham), 64 (Reinhard Dirscherl), 66 (Gerard Lacz), 68 (Malcolm Schuyl), 70 (Norbert Wu), 80 (Fred Bavendam), 86 (Silvestris Fotoservice), 90 (Reinhard Dirscherl)
Fotolia: 78 (Flipppi)
Getty Images: 40 (Barcroft Media), 76 (Brian J. Skerry)
iStockphoto: 30 (Tatiana Belova), 88 (Robin O'Connell)
Nature Picture Library: 22 (Bruce Rasner)
Photos.com: 50, 54, 58

Contents

Introduction

The oceans are a harsh and unforgiving environment, where often only the fastest, fittest, cleverest, and most cunning creatures make it through the day. Those that live long enough to mate and reproduce are the real winners in a shark-eat-shark world!

From the giant squid to the minuscule harlequin shrimp, each of the amazing animals you'll find in this book has its own way of exploiting its environment so that it comes out on top. Those with big teeth, huge jaws, and poisonous stingers have found one practical solution to the everyday problem of survival—be bigger and tougher than your rivals!

Other creatures have evolved more subtle survival techniques. Some are able to change their body shape and skin color to stay hidden out of harm's way. Some have toxic ink, paralyzing poison, or

MAKO SHARK

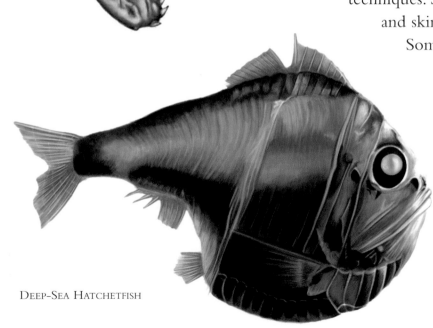

DEEP-SEA HATCHETFISH

jet-propulsion so they can make a quick getaway. And some have tough armor, spikes, and claws so that, if trouble does strike, they can meet it head on!

Many of these remarkable marine animals do indeed appear monstrous to human eyes. Take the deep-sea gulper eel (genus *Saccopharynx*), which is really little more than a mobile, extendable stomach, with a gaping maw at one end to sift the waters for food. Or the ugly hagfish (family Myxinidae), which suffocates its prey in a blanket of slime before eating it alive, from the inside out! Or the dead-eyed, great white shark (*Carcharodon carcharias*), which is one of the world's premier predators, and which—almost four decades after the movie *Jaws* was made—still fills us with dread. However, while it's easy to use emotive words like "monstrous," each of these animals is also a thing of beauty. In this book are creatures that have evolved over many millennia to be the best that they can be. Even if they're the best at being the baddest!

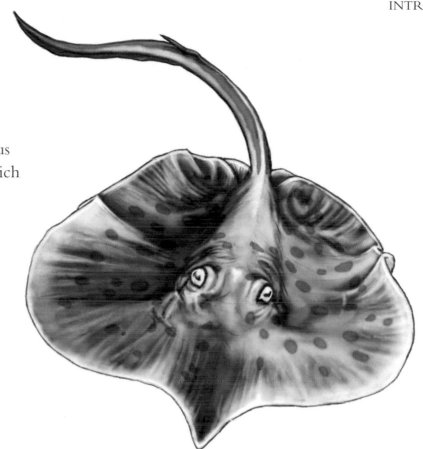

STINGRAY

CUTTLEFISH

Sharks

Before dinosaurs roamed the Earth, sharks were one of the ocean's top predators—one look at their teeth, and it's easy to understand why. The shape of a shark's teeth depends on the shark's diet: flat teeth crush bones and shells, while jagged edges saw through flesh. A shark's streamlined body also makes it a good hunter; the shortfin mako (*Isurus oxyrinchus*) reaches speeds of up to 45 mph (72 km/h). Yet not every shark is a flesh-eater or a speed fiend. Some are vegetarians, and others rely on camouflage and cunning.

There are many different species of shark that range in size from only a few inches to over 39 ft. (12 m). The Gray Reef Shark seen here grows to 4 ft. 10 in. (1.5 m).

Gray Reef Shark

COLORATION
As its name suggests, the upper body is gray, with a distinctive white underbelly.

SNOUT
The genus name *Carcharhinus* is Greek for *karcharos*, meaning "sharpen" and *rhinos*, meaning "nose."

TEETH
Dagger-like teeth in the shark's jaw have jagged (serrated) edges for gripping and cutting flesh.

BODY
The usual shape of a reef shark's body is long and stocky with a broad snout.

TAIL
Around the edge of the shark's tail (caudal fin) is a broad, black band.

They may be small, but these tropical terrors are no pushovers. Using aggressive "threat displays," gray reef sharks dominate the waters around coral reefs and warm, coastal bays. During the day, they're surprisingly sociable and gather together in groups, lazily circling their home range. As night approaches, though, lone hunters peel off from the group and move into shallower waters to feed. With bodies built for agility as well as speed, pursuing prey through the coral reefs is child's play for these sprightly sharks. Fish, squid, crab, and lobster are all on the menu, but divers beware! Gray reef sharks never attack without warning, but when they do, look out!

SIZE

Where in the world?

Gray reef sharks make their home in the Pacific and Indian oceans. They prefer warm, tropical waters, where they are often found cruising near coral reefs or in sheltered lagoons.

1. THIS GRAY REEF SHARK is being tagged by an over-curious diver. He'd better watch out. Reef sharks are quite sociable to other sharks, but they don't like being crowded by strangers.

2. HUNCHING ITS BACK and raising its snout, the shark swims forward, propelling its body through the water with a strange side-to-side motion. This odd behavior is a threat display and it means just one thing. Stay away!

3. THE DIVER IGNORES the warning signs. Big mistake! With its mouth open wide, the reef shark rushes in, gouging the diver's arm with its upper teeth. It then backs off, giving the diver the chance to make a rapid getaway.

Did you know?

● Male grays grow to about 4 ft. 10 in. (1.5 m). That's half the size of the hammerhead shark. However, they're quite able to chase their big cousins away.

● Female grays are viviparous: they give birth to live young, every other year. Usually one to six pups are born, but it can take seven years for these perfect little predators to develop fully.

● These incredible sharks have incredible noses! Their sense of smell is so good that they can detect one drop of tuna extract in every 10 billion drops of sea water.

● Gray reef sharks can go into feeding frenzies; when this happens, no one is safe! Other grays may even get eaten in the frantic rush to feed.

Sand Tiger Shark

COLORATION
Younger sharks can often be identified by reddish-brown spots scattered along their flanks, or sides.

LENGTH
These bulky sharks grow to a maximum size of about 10 ft. 5 in. (3.2 m).

SNOUT
A long, flattened snout holds a set of extendable jaws, which are used to engulf prey.

TAIL
The heterocercal tail fin is asymmetrical, with a much longer lobe above than below.

WEIGHT
A fully grown adult sand tiger can weigh as much as 640 lb. (290.3 kg).

Even with their jaws closed, rows of ragged teeth project at angles from this big shark's mighty mouth. However, it would be wrong to judge these fearsome-looking fish on appearances alone. They may be powerful predators, but they're surprisingly placid. They prey on a wide range of bony fish, sometimes working in small groups to surround a school before starting to feed. Where humans are concerned, they will attack only when trapped or provoked. Sadly, though, their ferocious appearance has done them no favors. In many parts of the world, hunters have decimated sand tiger populations, and it's only recently that these sharks have started to receive the protection they need.

SIZE

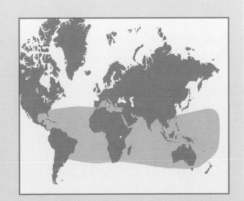

Where in the world?

Sand tiger sharks get their name from their habit of hugging the shoreline in search of food. They're found mainly in warm or temperate waters, except the Eastern Pacific.

SAND TIGERS START LIFE in a protective "sac," which contains nutrients to feed them. Once this is exhausted, instinct takes over. The biggest (and hungriest) embryo in each uterus survives by eating its siblings! These cannibalistic babies are only about 4 in. (10 cm) long, but they are amazingly aggressive. One researcher, dissecting a newly caught female, was even bitten by the unborn pup inside its mother's body!

Did you know?

● Sand tigers are the only species of shark that swim to the surface and gulp air. This is then stored in their stomachs, allowing them to float motionless in the water, when hunting.

● Sand tiger sharks are known by a wide range of popular names, including the gray nurse shark (in Australia) and the spotted ragged tooth shark (in South Africa).

● They may be slow swimmers, but these sharks have a clever technique for catching prey. They sometimes use their tails like whips, to herd fish into smaller areas.

● With pink skin, oversized heads, and rows of tiny needle-sharp teeth, embryo sand tigers look like something out of a science-fiction movie!

Great White Shark

DORSAL FIN
This characteristic fin stops the shark rolling, and helps it to make tight, fast turns.

BODY
A sleek, streamlined shape helps the great white to reach speeds of up to 40 mph (64.4 km/h).

TEETH
Rows of teeth behind the main set are ready to replace any that wear out.

TEMPERATURE
Closely packed veins and arteries help to maintain a body temperature warmer than the surrounding water.

AMPULLAE OF LORENZINI
Special sensing organs under the skin enable sharks to detect the electromagnetic fields emitted by living animals.

It's been almost four decades since the movie *Jaws* made us aware that, lurking in the ocean depths, was one of the world's premier predators. An average great white shark grows up to 13 ft. (4 m) long, although the largest specimens may be twice that size. Their rounded snout, torpedo-shaped body, and crescent tail make them superb swimmers. And rows of jagged-edged teeth enable them to shear chunks of flesh from their victims with ease. But, despite their impressive size and strength, these magnificent beasts are not cold, calculating killers. Unlike we humans, they kill only for food. They just happen to be very good at it!

SIZE

Where in the world?

Recent satellite tracking has shown that great whites migrate incredibly long distances, sometimes crossing entire oceans in search of prey. Although widespread, they are increasingly rare across their range.

1. GREAT WHITES OFTEN approach their prey, especially seals, from below. As they gather speed, they raise their snouts, thrusting their upper jaw forward. Ramming into their prey, they take a huge bite from their victim's body.

2. THESE GREAT SHARKS have no eyelids and so, to protect their eyes from damage, they roll them back into the socket as they bite down. The effect is chilling to watch.

3. SHARKS CAN'T CHEW. So, on impact, they lower their snout to bring both sets of jaws together. With the flesh firmly clamped between their teeth, they shake their head, using their body weight to pull off hunks of flesh. One bite is usually enough to leave their victim stunned and weak from blood loss.

Did you know?

● When hunting seals, great whites often launch breaching attacks—launching themselves up to 10 ft. (3.1 m) out of the water in pursuit of their prey.

● Great whites are one of the few species of shark that regularly pop their heads above the water line to see what's going on! This curious behavior is known as spy-hopping.

● Like many species of shark, great whites are ovoviviparous. Their eggs develop and hatch inside the mother's uterus. There, they continue to develop until the pup is ready to be born.

● The oldest known great white fossils are about 16 million years old. The oldest human remains that have so far been discovered are just 1.3 million years old.

Wobbegong

COLORATION
Wobbegongs and their
relatives are also known as
carpet sharks, thanks to their
striking camouflage.

EYES
A pair of hooded eyes are
surrounded by eye-shaped
markings, making them
difficult to spot.

JAWS
When prey is close, fang-
toothed jaws shoot out of the
wobbegong's flattened skull
with incredible speed.

TASSELS
An elaborate fringe of fleshy
tassels disguises the
wobbegong's outline, making
it even harder to see.

PECTORAL FINS
Enlarged pectoral fins are used
to help the wobbegong crawl
over the sea bed.

These amazingly camouflaged carpet sharks are masters of deception. With their flattened bodies, enlarged fins, and hooded eyes, these cunning hunters have no need of speed. They simply sit, on the ocean bottom, waiting for prey to pass by. It's only once a meal is within reach that the seemingly placid wobbegong shows its true colors. Within the blink of an eye, its tooth-lined jaws are propelled forward, impaling its prey. At the same time, the wobbegong's throat expands like a bellows, creating a powerful sucking action, which literally drags its victims into its mouth. Once that has happened, there's no escape from the clutches of this amazing ambush specialist.

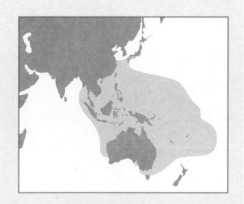

SIZE

No one knows exactly what wobbegong means, but it's generally translated as "living rock," which is what these remarkable creatures look like. During the day, they're happy to stay put, hidden amid the sand and seaweed. At night, however, they often forage for food. As well as all those tassels, they have sensitive nasal barbels, which they splay out, like cats' whiskers, to help find food.

Did you know?

● Wobbegongs have big families. The spotted wobbegong (*Orectolobus maculatus*) may have as many as 37 pups in one litter.

● Even a fish, asleep in a rock crevice, stands little chance of escaping a determined wobbegong. The clever hunter simply presses its head over the rock opening and sucks them out!

● Sadly, the wonderfully patterned skin that makes the wobbegong such a good hunter has, in turn, caused it to become hunted. Its skin is highly sought-after by manufacturers of sharkskin purses, belts, and bags.

● Wobbegongs have no interest in humans, but they will bite if disturbed. Despite their small teeth, such bites can be very nasty, as the shark often shuts its jaws on its victim.

Where in the world?

Wobbegongs make their homes on coral reefs, under piers, and in sandy-bottomed, shallow waters. Most species are found around Australia and islands in the Pacific and the South China Sea.

Horn Shark

SPINES
The horn shark is named for the two prominent spines in front of each dorsal fin.

HEAD
A short, wide head and blunt snout give this group its common name—bullhead sharks.

PECTORAL FINS
Strong pectoral fins help the horn shark to push itself along the sea bottom.

BODY
Adult horn sharks grow to about 3 ft. 2 in. (1 m). Some may grow to 4 ft. (1.2 m).

TEETH
Adults have crushing teeth near the rear of the jaw and conical, grasping teeth at the front.

With their pudgy bodies, puckered lips, and perplexed expressions, it's hard to believe that these mollusk-munchers really are sharks. While other members of the super-order Selachimorpha are sleek, speedy, and savage, horn sharks are almost cute! By day, they doze on the sea bottom. At night, they set off, with a clumsy wiggle, in search of food. Some dine on mollusks or sea urchins, crushing the spines and shells with their molar-like teeth. Others use that pursed mouth to suck up fish. Their small size and slow movements make them natural targets for larger predators, but they're no pushovers. Those spines are big enough to slash any would-be attacker.

SIZE

Where in the world?

Bullhead sharks are found in the warm waters of the eastern Pacific and western Indian Ocean. Favorite resting and hunting spots are sandy bottoms, rocky outcrops, caves, and kelp beds.

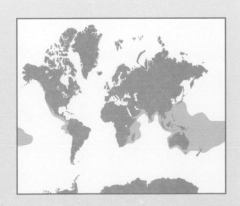

1. THIS BABY HORN SHARK isn't as helpless as it looks. The dorsal "horns" for which the species is named make surprisingly good weapons, as one predator is just about to discover!

2. HIDDEN BENEATH THE SAND, lurks a hungry angel shark, waiting patiently for some unsuspecting victim to pass by. As the horn shark approaches, this angel reacts with devilish speed! Snapping up its head, the predator throws open its jaws and sucks in the unsuspecting juvenile.

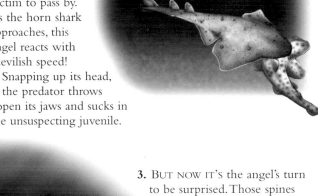

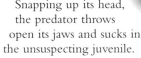

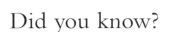

3. BUT NOW IT'S the angel's turn to be surprised. Those spines make a prickly mouthful and the hunter reluctantly spits out his hoped-for meal, leaving the lucky horn shark to swim to freedom.

Did you know?

● Horn sharks have a varied diet, but are especially fond of red sea urchins. They often eat so many that their teeth are stained red.

● The horn shark's diet includes crustaceans and mollusks. Such hard-shelled prey presents no problems for these bullheads. They simply grind up their food—shell and all—and regurgitate (spit out) the hard parts later.

● Most sharks die within a few days of being captured, but these thick-set beasts seem to cope well with captivity. This means that they are one of the few shark species that can be kept in aquariums.

● Those formidable-looking "horns" make great defensive weapons. Predators who manage to get a horn shark in their mouth often quickly spit them out again!

Mako Shark

COLORATION
Makos are strikingly colored —deep purple on the upper body (the dorsal surface), with silvery sides.

BODY: SHORTFIN
Shortfin makos (*Isurus oxyrinchus*) grow to between 6 and 8 ft. (1.8–2.4 m) long.

BODY: LONGFIN
The second species of mako, the longfin (*I. paucus*), grows to about 7 ft. (2.1 m).

PECTORAL FINS
Long pectoral fins on either side of the shark's body act like stabilizers when they swim.

TAIL
Most fish have a homocercal tail; this is a tail that extends beyond the backbone and that is almost symmetrical.

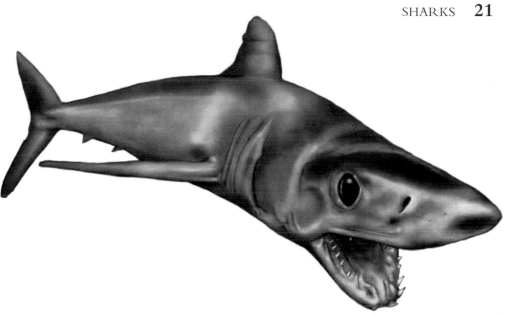

I f you could distil the "essence of shark" into just one species, the result would be the mako. These breathtakingly beautiful fish are an amazing combination of raw power and streamlined style. Among anglers, they're known as Blue Dynamite thanks to their explosive bursts of speed and ability to leap at least 20 ft. (6.1 m) into the air. In the oceans, these hunters sit at the very top of the food chain, feeding on some of the world's fastest and most aggressive marine species, including blue sharks, billfish, dolphins, tuna, and mackerel. But when they're annoyed, watch out! They'll even tackle objects above the water line, including boats!

SIZE

IT WAS THE AMERICAN author Zane Gray (1872–1939) who helped propel the mako shark to fame with his exciting descriptions of it. Despite being an experienced hunter, Zane once commented that he "was never so scared as by this beast." Today, however, we are learning to appreciate that makos are more than just powerful and aggressive creatures; they are also highly intelligent.

Did you know?

● Like their cousins, the great whites, makos can keep their body temperature warmer than the surrounding water. This gives them a huge advantage when pursuing prey, as their muscles are already warm.

● According to the International Shark Attack File, a total of 29 attacks (from the year when records began to 2010) have been attributed to the mako.

● The shortfin mako is probably the world's fastest shark. During the pursuit of prey, these amazing athletes are capable of bursts of speed up to 45 mph (72.4 km/h).

● Captured makos often bear scars from too-close encounters with swordfish. One mako found by fishermen had been stabbed through the eye by the bill of a swordfish.

Where in the world?

Makos like to stay warm. They are found around the world, in tropical and temperate oceans, but are rarely seen in waters that are less than 61°F (16.1°C).

Megamouth Shark

TAIL
The caudal tail fin is asymmetrical, with a much longer lobe above than below.

BODY
The shark's stocky body and wide snout ends in that very wide and long "megamouth."

GILLS
Lining the megamouth shark's gills are specialized "filters" that strain the food from the water.

MOUTH
The upper jaw contains sheets of silvery tissue, but it's now known that the mouth is not bioluminescent.

TONGUE
The shark's basihyal (tongue) is particularly large and very flexible. This may help it feed.

The ocean is our planet's last, great frontier. More people have stood on the surface of the Moon than have traveled to the lowest point of the ocean. So, it is not surprising that this great, unexplored wilderness occasionally yields something incredible. This happened in 1976, when a U.S. naval ship discovered something very strange caught on its sea anchor. Scientists dubbed it megamouth, for obvious reasons! Since then, this deep-sea dweller has proved to be extremely elusive. Only 49 specimens of these rubbery-mouthed oddities have so far been found, but every one that can be examined reveals new information about these strangest of all sharks.

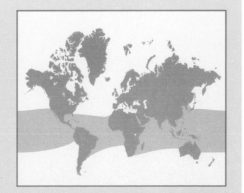

SIZE

Where in the world?

Although there have been only 50 confirmed sightings, this species is now known to inhabit the Indian, Pacific, and Atlantic oceans. Most sightings have been off the coast of Japan.

1. TO GET ENOUGH FOOD, it's likely that the megamouth is a vertical migrator, constantly moving up and down through the water. Usually, vertical migrators move up to the epipelagic zone (the illuminated surface) at night. During the day, they return to the mesopelagic zone, to a depth of about 3,300 ft. (1,006 m).

2. FEEDING IN THE WARM surface waters at night and resting in the cooler, deeper waters during the day may help the megamouth save energy. Feeding at night may also simply be safer. At least one megamouth sighting suggests that whales prey on them; observers noticed injuries on megamouth's fins and gills that suggested a whale attack.

Did you know?

● Megamouth can grow up to 18 ft. (5.5 m) long. To fuel such a huge body, it needs a lot of food, but, surprisingly, this big fish is not a big game hunter. It's a filter feeder and most of its diet consists of tiny, planktonic animals, which it strains from the water.

● Megamouth is one of the three known, giant filter-feeding sharks. The other two are the basking shark (*Cetorhinus maximus*) and the whale shark (*Rhincodon typus*).

● These sharks are surprisingly slow and sluggish. It is estimated that megamouth swims at about 0.9–1.3 mph (1.4–2.1 km/h).

● Megamouth belongs to the genus *Megachasma*. This name is from the Greek *megas*, meaning "great," and *chasma*, meaning "cave."

Whale Shark

GILLS
Lining the whale shark's gills are specialized "filters" that strain the food from the water.

TEETH
Around 27,000 teeth are arranged in 300 rows inside the mouth. They have no known use!

SKIN
Whale sharks have the thickest skin of any animal—6 in. (15.2 cm) thick in places!

THROAT
Powerful throat muscles are used like a bellows to pump food-bearing water over the "filters."

EYES
Whale sharks don't hunt for food, and have few enemies, so they don't need good vision.

Everything about the whale shark is big. This remarkable record breaker is the world's largest living shark as well as the largest living fish. These incredible creatures grow up to 45 ft. (13.7 m) long, and can weigh as much as 13 tons (11.6 tonnes). Their mouths alone are a whopping 6 ft. (1.8 m) across—big enough to gulp down three percent of their body weight in food in one sitting. As well as eating planktonic (microscopic) prey, whale sharks will also take nektonic (larger free-swimming) species, including fish and squid, when they get the chance. However, unlike their smaller cousins, these sharks are real gentle giants.

THIS BIG MOUTH HAS ONLY ONE JOB to do: to suck in as much water as possible. Once the mouth is closed, the water is forced out again, through the shark's gills. Spongy plates between the gill bars (the structures that support the gills) filter out anything larger than a few millimeters. So, the food stays in and the water goes out!

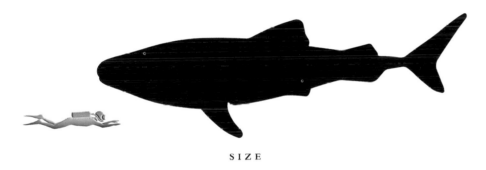

SIZE

Did you know?

● Although whale sharks have 300 rows of teeth, they no longer use them. Instead, they filter their food from the surrounding water. On average they can filter 400,000 gallons (1.5 million liters) of water per hour.

● The whale shark's distinctive stripes and dots have earned it the nickname "checkerboard shark." These light yellow markings are even more dramatic set against the fish's dark gray skin.

● Most sharks swim by propelling themselves forward with side-to-side sweeps of their powerful tail. In contrast, whale sharks move their entire bodies from side to side.

● It takes a long time to grow this big. Male whale sharks don't reach adulthood until they are 30, when they start to breed. They may live to be over 100.

Where in the world?

These gigantic filter feeders prefer warm waters where plankton flourishes. They are frequently seen close to the shore, sometimes entering lagoons or coral reefs where food is more plentiful.

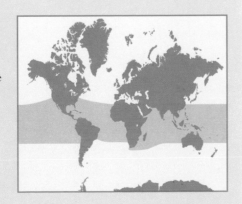

Hammerhead Shark

HEAD
This strange hammer shape is known, scientifically, as a cephalofoil. All hammerheads share this distinctive feature.

COLORATION
Hammerheads are usually light greenish-gray with pale bellies. If exposed to sunlight, they may tan.

EYES
Eyes at either end of the "hammer" help these hunters to judge distances more accurately.

PECTORAL FINS
These fins, on either side of the body, help sharks steer and move up and down.

These huge heads may look silly, but they have a very serious purpose. Thanks to specialized organs under the skin, called ampullae of Lorenzini, sharks can detect the electrical signals produced by the bodies of living animals. The hammer shape spreads these organs over a much wider area. So, by sweeping its head back and forth over the sandy sea bottom, the hammerhead can home in on tell-tale "signals" from its prey. The hammerhead's eyes are positioned at either end of its "hammer," which gives it a very wide field of vision. And because its nostrils are at either end of the hammer, it can sniff out prey much more easily.

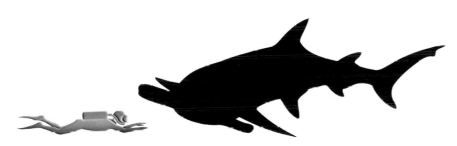

SIZE

Where in the world?

Hammerhead sharks make their homes in the world's tropical and subtropical waters. They are frequently seen around coastlines, where they often gather together in shoals of 100 or more sharks.

1. HAMMERHEADS ENJOY a varied diet. Fish, squid, octopus, crustaceans, and even other species of hammerhead shark are on the menu, but stingrays are a particular favorite. Most stingrays have one or more barbed stings on their tail, but this doesn't seem to deter hungry hammerheads. In fact, one Great Hammerhead, which was caught off Florida, had an incredible 96 barbs embedded in its mouth!

2. ONCE THE HAMMERHEAD is sure of its victim's location, it moves in. Rays are agile and swift, but just as the stingray looks like it might make a clean getaway, the shark swings its hammer-like club, pinning the stingray down. Twisting around, the shark quickly moves in for the kill.

Did you know?

● Native Hawaiians used to believe that they were watched over by protective animal spirits known as *aumakua*. *Aumakua* take many forms, including hammerhead sharks.

● The largest of the hammerheads is the great hammerhead (*Sphyrna mokarran*); the largest of these measured about 20 ft. (6.1 m) long.

● The hammerhead's skin is covered in tiny, diamond-shaped spikes called dermal denticles. In the eighteenth century, sharkskin (known as shagreen) was often used on sword hilts and was highly valued because the rough surface gave a good grip.

● Hammerheads are viviparous: they give birth to live young. One litter can range in size from 6 to about 50 pups. At birth, the pups have more rounded heads; they develop the characteristic hammer only as they mature.

Angel Shark

BODY
Like rays, angel sharks are dorsoventrally flattened (squashed along the length of their back).

COLORATION
Angel sharks vary in color from blue-gray to almost white. Irregular spots provide additional camouflage.

PECTORAL FINS
These elongated fins almost look like wings, which is why they are called angel sharks.

SPIRACLE
Small holes behind each eye help the shark breathe. These are larger in bottom-dwelling sharks.

EYES
Eyes on the top of the head enable the shark to see when it is buried in sand.

SHARKS **29**

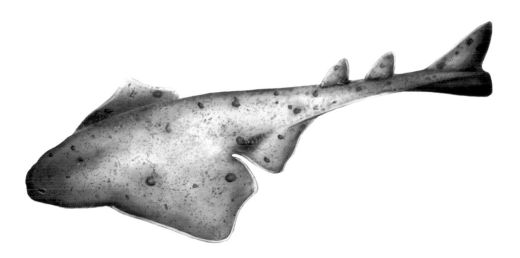

These flat-bodied sharks may look harmless, but looks can be deceptive. Their only true "angelic virtue" is patience! It may take weeks for potential prey to wander past, but angel sharks are happy to while away their time buried in the mud or sand on the sea bed. When some unfortunate fish or squid finally does stray a little too close, then these sea-bed terrors are no sluggards. They react with lightning speed. Snapping up their head and shooting out their trap-like jaws, they quickly suck in their helpless victim. In fact, their sharp teeth and powerful bite have earned this group of sharks another, less angelic, nickname: sand devils.

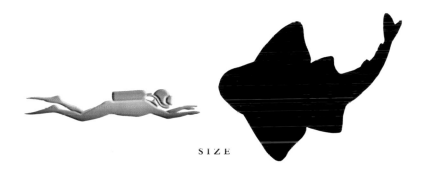

SIZE

ANGEL SHARKS BREATHE using a method called buccal pumping, named for the buccal (cheek) muscles. These muscles suck water into the mouth. As it's hard to do this with their mouths buried in the sand, they have larger spiracles than other shark species. These act like a "spare" mouth to pull in water. The water exits through the gills, which is where the oxygen is removed.

Where in the world?

This widespread group can be found in coastal areas of most of the world's oceans, from cool, temperate waters to tropical zones. They spend much of their time on the sandy bottom.

Did you know?

● Little is known about these surprisingly secretive sharks. In fact, scientists disagree as to exactly how many species there are—probably between 16 and 19.

● In England, angel sharks are also known as monkfish. Until recently, they were a popular dish in fish and chip shops, where they were served, fried in batter. Many people now avoid eating monkfish because of concerns about overfishing.

● The Latin name for this group of sharks is Squatina. This might sound like a reference to its "squat," flattened shape, but it means "a kind of shark."

● These ambush specialists generally grow to only about 5 ft. (1.5 m) long, although the Japanese angel shark (*Squatina japonica*) measures about 6 ft. 6 in. (2 m) long.

Other Saltwater Fish

About 71 percent of our planet is covered by saltwater, which is home to at least 230,000 species. We may know only one-tenth of the plants and animals living in the oceans, but of the species we do know, many are surprising, even shocking. Take, for example, the frogfish (genus *Antennatus*), which enlarges its mouth up to 12 times its normal size to grab prey. Or the hagfish (family Myxinidae), which eats its victims from the inside out! The world's saltwater fish are as variable as the oceans themselves.

Life on Earth began in the seas, and it remains a place of great variety and wonder. The oceans, at depths of almost 9,800 ft. (3,000 m), are still relatively unexplored, and it is thought that there are many more species to be discovered.

Spotted Eagle Ray

SPIRACLES
When the ray's mouth is buried in the sand, holes behind each eye help it breathe.

EYES
A pair of large eyes gives the ray excellent vision in the gloomy ocean depths.

BODY
Rays are dorsoventrally flattened, which means that they are squashed along the length of their back.

SPINES
These venomous spines can deliver a nasty sting when used to defend the ray against predators.

PECTORAL FINS
The eagle ray is part of the order Batoidea, and like most batoids it swims by undulating or flapping its enlarged pectoral fins, like wings.

Possibly one of the most beautiful of the rays, the spotted eagle sports a striking pattern of pearl, bluish, and yellowish spots across its dark, blue-gray upper body. Its tail tapers into a long whip, while an upturned snout and a duck-like bill complete its unique profile. Such a dramatic body has many advantages. It not only helps the ray hide from predators, but also keeps it well hidden when it is on the hunt itself. Lying motionless beneath the sand and mud, the spotted eagle is almost invisible. But once it's on the move, it's like a creature from another world—a fish that swims as though flying through water.

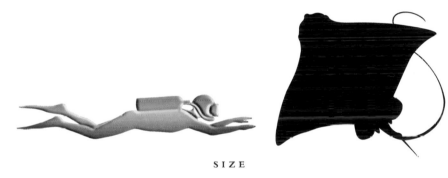

SIZE

Where in the world?

Spotted eagle rays are found in the world's warm tropical and cooler temperate waters. They are usually seen in small shoals in shallow coastal waters, around coral reefs and sandy bays.

1. A TRAWLER MAN GUIDES in his latest catch—a net filled to bursting point with thousands of flapping fish, freshly scooped from the sea bed. But, hidden amid the catch, there's a nasty surprise. A spotted eagle ray has been caught up in the net and is frantically trying to free itself.

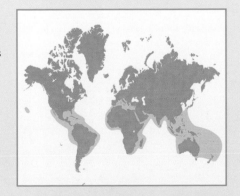

2. THE TRAWLER MAN HASN'T noticed the ray's distinctive, whip-like tail poking through the net's mesh. He's far too busy working. As he moves in to secure the catch, the ray thrashes out, embedding its barbed spines deep in the trawler man's wrist. Every ray carries two to six spines at the base of its tail, and these can cause agonizing wounds.

Did you know?

● The largest spotted eagle rays have a maximum disk width of 9 ft. 10 in. (3 m) and weigh in at about 507 lb. (230 kg).

● That whip-like tail can be as long as the ray's entire body. While the stinging spines (just behind the dorsal fin) are relatively short, they are extremely dangerous, with a barbed tip and "teeth" along their length.

● The eagle's stubby snout is used to root in the mud for food like mollusks and invertebrates. It's because of this odd feature that eagle rays are sometimes known as duck-billed rays.

● Although sharks, particularly hammerheads (family Sphyrnidae), prey on rays, the two species are very closely related and have the same common ancestor. In fact, rays are really like "flattened" sharks!

Atlantic Wolf Fish

DORSAL FIN
A long dorsal fin runs along the wolf's whole back. This helps stabilize its body.

TEETH
The wolf fish gets its common name from its four to six fang-like, conical teeth.

SKIN
The skin appears smooth and slippery. Colors vary from purplish-brown to a dull, olive gray.

BODY
The largest recorded specimen of wolf fish measured in at almost 5 ft. (1.5 m) long.

With its long scaleless body and bulbous head, this cold-loving species looks more like an eel than a fish. Its preferred prey are crustaceans, mollusks, and starfish, which it makes short work of in its powerful jaws. In fact, thanks to its large teeth, it is able to eat its prey whole—shells and all—by ripping its victim's body into small, manageable chunks. It may be slow, but it has one huge advantage over other bottom-dwellers. Most fish hunt by tracking their prey using sound or vibrations, but these water wolves have big eyes. Placed well forward on the top of their head, these give the wolf superb vision in the gloomy depths.

SIZE

Where in the world?

These hardy fish make their homes in the world's coldest oceans, around Northern Europe and North America. They're found on sea beds or rocky caverns, at depths as low as 1,650 ft. (503 m).

MALE WOLF FISH ARE SURPRISING SOFTIES. The usual way for most fish to reproduce is for the females to drop their eggs in the ocean. Males fertilize them, then move on, leaving the young to hatch alone and undefended. Male wolf fish, though, actually build a "nest" and stay to protect the developing young for up to four months, until they can survive on their own.

Did you know?

● Atlantic wolf fish are a benthic species, which means that they live on or near the sea bed.

● It's not unusual to find wolf fish living in temperatures as low as 34-37°F (1.1-2.8°C). To stop their bodies from freezing, the blood of wolf fish contains a natural "antifreeze"!

● The wolf fish, or sea cat as it is sometimes called, is a very ancient species that has been found in fossil records dating back over 50 million years.

● Wolf fish prey on invasive "non-native" species, such as green crabs (*Carcinus maenas*) and sea urchins (class Echinoidea). So without these important predators at the top of the food chain, many vital ecosystems, especially coral beds, would be destroyed by these aggressive newcomers.

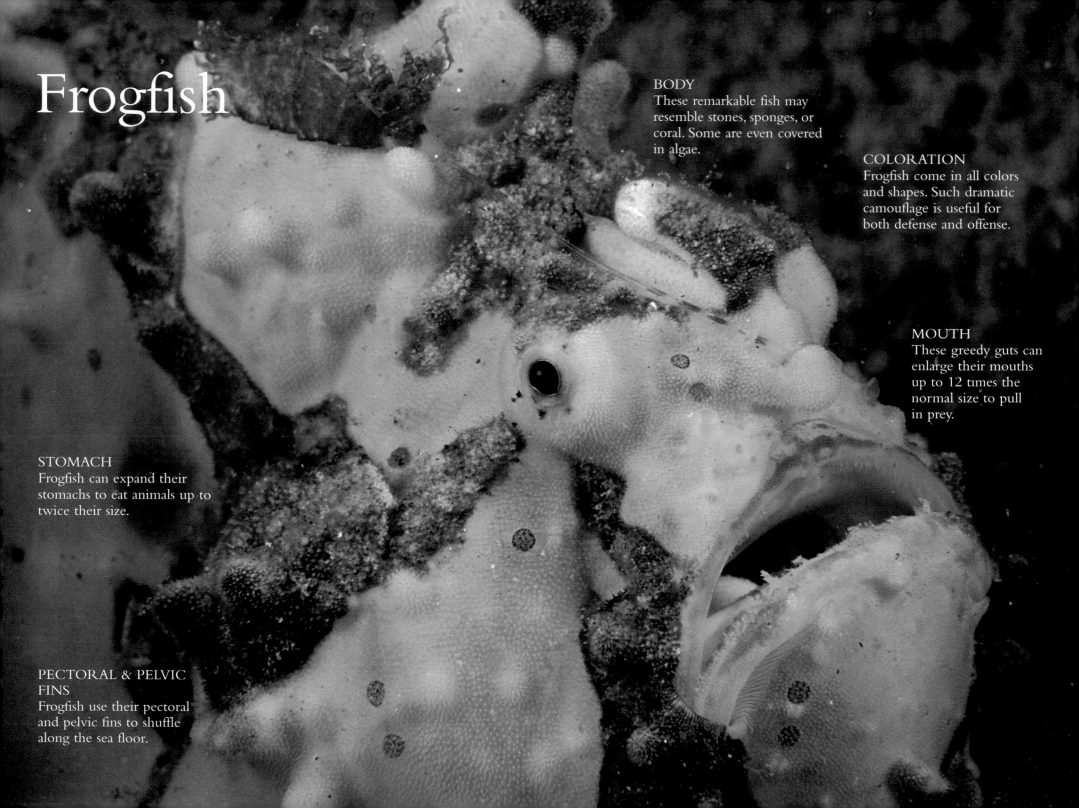

Frogfish

BODY
These remarkable fish may resemble stones, sponges, or coral. Some are even covered in algae.

COLORATION
Frogfish come in all colors and shapes. Such dramatic camouflage is useful for both defense and offense.

MOUTH
These greedy guts can enlarge their mouths up to 12 times the normal size to pull in prey.

STOMACH
Frogfish can expand their stomachs to eat animals up to twice their size.

PECTORAL & PELVIC FINS
Frogfish use their pectoral and pelvic fins to shuffle along the sea floor.

These freaky-looking fish are one of the ocean's great mimics. Their unusual shape, color, and skin texture is all part of their incredible camouflage. As they have no scales, being able to blend in with the background is a great defense against more aggressive species. However, it's also very useful when hunting! Frogfish aren't great swimmers, but they don't need to be. They can simply lie in wait, looking like innocent pieces of rock or some algae, until a meal swims by. And just to help things along, they come equipped with their own fishing rod and a pair of powerful jaws to suck up any passing prey.

SIZE

Where in the world?

These fantastic fish can be found in the tropical and subtropical waters of the Atlantic, Pacific, and Indian oceans. They prefer water that is at least 68°F (20°C).

1. MOST FISH HAVE at least one dorsal fin on their back. This acts like a stabilizer to stop them rolling over. However, in frogfish, the frontmost dorsal fin is adapted for a very special purpose—fishing!

2. THIS DORSAL FIN (called an illicium) acts like a rod and line to lure in prey. What's more, every illicium is different, depending on the species of frogfish. Some look like fish, some like shrimp, some like tube worms, depending on the frogfish's preferred prey.

3. ONCE THEIR PREY has taken the bait, there's no escape! The frogfish's jaws spring open, pulling the prey into their mouth so fast that it's almost impossible to see.

Did you know?

● It takes just six milliseconds for a frogfish to suck in its prey. In fact, it's only by using slow-motion cameras that it's possible to see this happen!

● Females may lay as many as 180,000 eggs. Generally these are released into the open ocean, although in the case of the male three-spot frogfish (*Lophiocharon trisignatus*) egg clusters stay attached to the side of his body until they hatch.

● Should a frogfish lose its lure, it simply grows another one! This can take up to six months.

● Some frogfish can inflate themselves, like puffer fish (family Tetraodontidae), by sucking in water. This is a threat display, intended to make them look bigger and more impressive to any potential predators.

Deep-Sea Hatchetfish

EYES
Large eyes can collect all available light and focus well on objects both near and far.

BODY
The body is flattened and shaped like an ax (hatchet), which gives the group its common name.

MOUTH
The mouth is at the tip of the snout and points upward to catch falling food.

FINS
Fins are small. This reduces the fish's body weight and so the need for food.

PHOTOPHORES
Light-producing organs are dotted along the fish's distinctively shaped underbelly, giving out a blue glow.

Food in the deep oceans is scarce, so hatchetfish are adapted to make the most of what's available. These small, compact fish come with huge gaping mouths, which they use to suck up the debris that filters down from the waters above. To help them search for food, their large, luminous eyes point upward, scanning the depths for a tasty treat. However, the ocean is full of hungry hunters, so hatchets stay safe using photophores dotted along their bellies. These give out an eerie light, which can be adjusted to match the level of sun filtering from above. This helps them to blend in with their surroundings and to hunt almost invisibly.

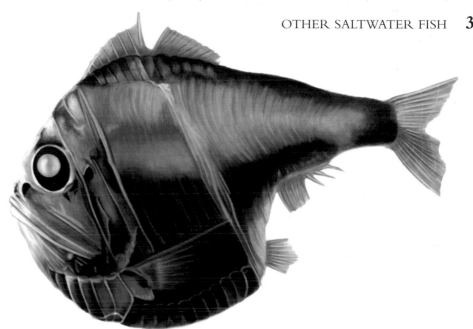

SIZE

Where in the world?

Hatchetfish are mesopelagic, which means that they can be found in the deep oceans, at depths of between 650 and 3,300 ft. (198–1,006 m). They are more common in cooler, food-rich waters.

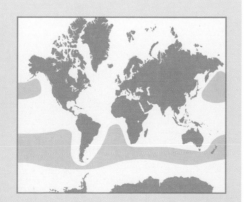

IT MIGHT SEEM ODD FOR A FISH living in the deep, dark oceans to draw attention to itself by putting on a light show. However, many fish hunt their prey from below. In fact, the hatchet spends much of its time looking "up" in order to spot the outlines of fish moving against the brighter upper waters. So counterillumination actually helps camouflage the hatchet by disrupting its silhouette.

Did you know?

● Deep-sea hatchetfish belong to a large marine subfamily known as Sternoptychinae. The name comes from the Greek for "breast crease," which is a reference to the fish's compressed body shape.

● Within this large group, there are at least 40 different species. Deep-sea fish are hard to find, though, so there may be many more species yet to be discovered.

● Some species, like the highlight hatchetfish (*Sternoptyx pseudobscura*), have taken camouflage to a whole new level and are almost completely transparent.

● Members of the genus *Argyropelecus* are also known as silver hatchetfish because of the way that their bodies seem to shimmer and shine in the water. Their silvery scales help to reflect light and further disrupt their silhouette.

Viperfish

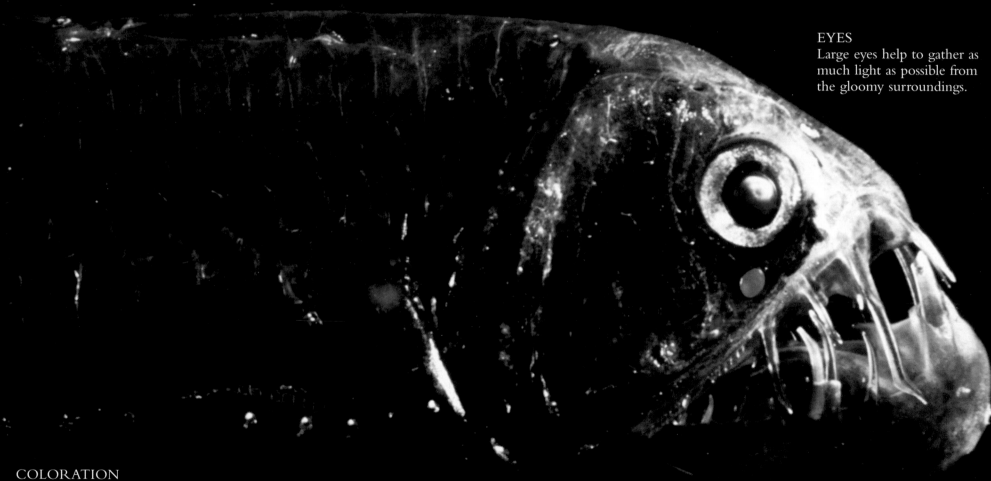

DORSAL FIN
The elongated dorsal fin is used like a fisherman's lure, to pull in prey.

EYES
Large eyes help to gather as much light as possible from the gloomy surroundings.

COLORATION
Scales have a silvery shimmer, which reflect light and disrupt the fish's silhouette.

PHOTOPHORES
Light-producing organs are dotted along the fish's belly, giving out an eerie blue glow.

TEETH
When its mouth is closed, these impressive fangs curve over the top of the viper's head.

With its eel-like body, flip-top jaws, and massive fangs, this deep-sea dweller is a truly nightmarish vision. Fortunately, there are few who have seen this predator up close, as it lives in the mesopelagic zone, at depths of between 650 and 3,300 ft. (198–1,006 m). There, in the cool, dark waters, food is so scarce that the viperfish has had to evolve some very curious features to survive. These include an in-built fishing rod, tipped with a luminous lure, to attract food. The viper's underbelly is also dotted with light-producing photophores. These emit a faint counterillumination, which disrupts the viper's silhouette and helps it hide from bigger predators.

SIZE

Where in the world?

Viperfish can be found throughout the world's oceans, in tropical and temperate zones. It's likely that they are vertical migrators, constantly moving up and down through the water to find food.

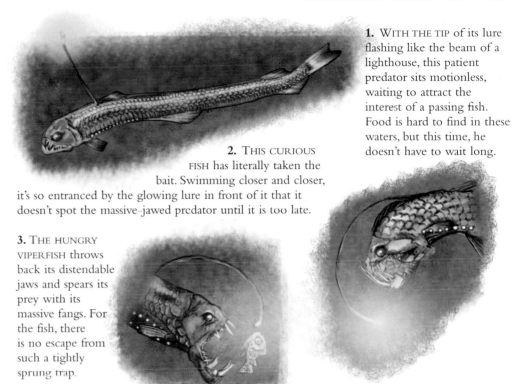

1. WITH THE TIP of its lure flashing like the beam of a lighthouse, this patient predator sits motionless, waiting to attract the interest of a passing fish. Food is hard to find in these waters, but this time, he doesn't have to wait long.

2. THIS CURIOUS FISH has literally taken the bait. Swimming closer and closer, it's so entranced by the glowing lure in front of it that it doesn't spot the massive-jawed predator until it is too late.

3. THE HUNGRY VIPERFISH throws back its distendable jaws and spears its prey with its massive fangs. For the fish, there is no escape from such a tightly sprung trap.

Did you know?

● Viperfish have hinged jaws, which they can open at an angle of more than 90 degrees. Perfect for gulping down prey!

● The first vertebra behind the viperfish's head is twice the size of the one next to it. This acts like a shock absorber to cope with the sudden force of the viper throwing open its jaws.

● Vipers can adjust the amount of light given out by their photophores to match the level of sunlight that filters down through the water from the world above. This helps it to blend in with its surroundings.

● Vipers may also use their photophores to communicate with other members of their species—warning rivals to stay away, or inviting potential mates to come closer!

Porcupine Fish

JAWS
A pair of beak-like jaws are used to crush the shells of crustaceans and mollusks.

FINS
Small fins don't generate much speed, but they help the fish make fine maneuvers.

BODY: UNDER THREAT
When trouble strikes, porcupines inflate their bodies like balloons. This pushes their spines upright.

BODY: AT REST
Normally, porcupines are more recognizably fish-shaped and their spines lie flat against their bodies.

SPINES
These bony spines are modified scales. They can grow up to 2 in. (5.1 cm) long.

These spherical fish have a surprising way of dealing with
trouble. They gulp down water until their stomachs look
like overinflated balloons. Their bodies don't get any longer,
just rounder! As they inflate, the long, bony spines that usually lie
flat along their bodies are pushed up and out—making this little fish
big trouble for any hungry hunter. This is such an effective
technique that porcupine fish have few enemies. In fact, the
naturalist Charles Darwin (1809-1882) recorded in his journals that
porcupine fish were known to inflate themselves in the mouths of
sharks. Once their attacker had choked to death, they simply
chewed their way out of the body!

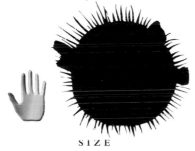

SIZE

MEMBERS OF THE GENUS *DIODON* share three main characteristics. First, they have long, sharp
spines embedded in their skin. Second, their teeth are fused together, to create a beak-like
mouth, which is ideal for crushing shells. Finally, their fins are greatly reduced in size. This
means that they can't reach great speeds when swimming, but can make precise maneuvers in
and out of coral reefs.

Did you know?

● Porcupine fish are also known as globe fish or balloon fish, for very obvious reasons!

● All porcupine fish are capable of inflating their bodies, but some species can also change their
color to blend in with their surroundings. This is believed to be a defense mechanism.

● Charles Darwin recorded in his journals how the porcupine fish reacted to threat: it "could
give a severe bite ... could eject water from its mouth to some distance ... But the most curious
circumstance was that it emitted from the skin of its belly, when handled, a most beautiful
carmine red."

● Some species of porcupine fish are extremely poisonous. Their bodies contain a neurotoxin
that is at least 1,200 times more deadly than cyanide.

Where in the world?

Porcupine fish are most at home in the
warm waters—they're circumtropical.
They are most commonly found nestling
amid coral reefs or sea grass beds, at
depths as low as 328 ft. (100 m).

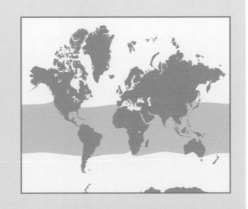

Deep-Sea Gulper Eel

SIZE
Members of the genus *Saccopharynx* can grow up to 6 ft. 6 in. (2 m) long.

MOUTH
Gulpers use their massive mouths like fishing nets to scoop up any passing prey.

TEETH
Rows of tiny, needle-sharp teeth are useful for gripping on to wet, wriggling fish.

BODY
Gulpers' bodies are like big empty sacks. In fact, *Saccopharynx* comes from the Latin *saccus,* meaning "sack."

LURE
Tapering tails end in a glowing bulb-shaped organ, which probably acts like a fishing lure.

Gulper eels are really little more than mobile, extendable stomachs, with a gaping maw at one end to sift the waters for food. This vast mouth accounts for two-thirds of the gulper's body length and is generally lined with needle-sharp teeth. At the other end is a tapered tail, which contains a glowing, bioluminescent "lure" to attract prey. Unfortunately, finding enough food to fill such a big mouth is tricky in the deep oceans that gulpers call home. So, its body has been pared down to the bare essentials to save energy. It has no scales, it is narrow with small fins and a thin tail, and it has massively reduced muscles and internal organs.

SIZE

Where in the world?

Little is known about the habits of these deep-sea creatures, but it's believed they live in the warmer waters of the world's oceans, at depths of up to 10,000 ft. (3,048 m).

1. THIS LITTLE FISH is in for a big surprise. Entranced by an eerie, pulsating glow in the gloom, it moves in to take a better look. Perhaps there's something good to eat?

2. COILED UP LIKE A GIANT underwater python, the gulper opens its huge mouth and a deadly game of cat and mouse begins. Moving its lure in front of its mouth, the gulper entices the little fish ever closer.

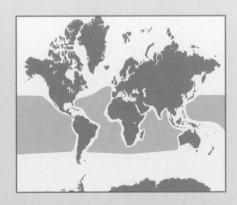

3. OBLIVIOUS TO THE DANGER—and with its eyes fixed on the tasty-looking lure—the fish swims into the gulper's cavernous maw. It's all over in a few seconds. At these depths, food is hard to find, and it's eat or be eaten!

Did you know?

● It is believed that the gulper's lure may also be used to attract a mate, as finding a partner in the watery gloom must be an extremely tricky process!

● Deep-sea gulpers are inhabitants of the aphotic zone, where little or no sunlight filters down from the waters above. This probably makes its glowing lure look even more enticing.

● As with most deep-sea species, scientists have been able to study only dead or dying specimens that have been accidentally caught in trawlers' nets. So, there is still much to learn about these elusive creatures.

Chimaera

SPINE
For protection, many chimaeras have a poisonous spine just in front of the dorsal fin.

SKIN
Like their distant cousins, the sharks and rays, chimaeras have skins that are covered by rough dermal denticles.

SNOUT: FAMILY CALLORHINCHIDAE
The plownose chimaera, or elephantfish as it is also called, has an unusual, flexible, plow-shaped snout.

SNOUT: FAMILY RHINOCHIMAERIDAE
This group is also called the long-nose chimaera due to their elongated, pointed snout.

SNOUT: FAMILY CHIMAERIDAE
Also known as the short-nose chimaera (shown), this group can be recognized by the rounded snout.

The three families of fish within the order Chimaeriformes each have their own special adaptations that enable them to survive at different ocean depths, without competing directly with each other for food. The plownoses (family Callorhinchidae) prefer shallower coastal waters, where they use that upturned snout to root for mollusks and crustaceans in the sea bed. The short-noses (family Chimaeridae) live farther down, so they have larger eyes to spot prey in the dark. The long-noses (family Rhinochimaeridae) live even farther down in the murky depths, up to 6,600 ft. (2,012 m). There, that long, sensitive snout is the ideal tool to help them search for prey in the dark.

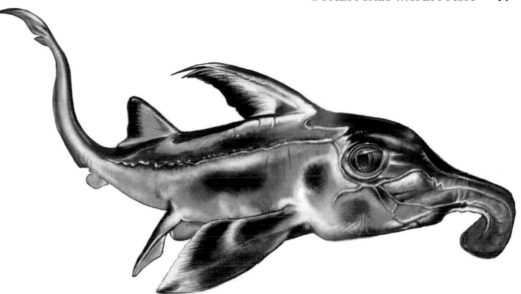

WITH THEIR STRANGE SNOUTS AND UNGAINLY WAY OF MOVING, chimaeras look curiously comic, but these funny fish are one of nature's great survivors. Fossilized remains of this ancient animal date back 400 million years. Their closest living relatives are the sharks, but while their cousins became sleek super-predators, chimaera bodies adapted to suit a very different lifestyle.

SIZE

Did you know?

● In the famous ancient Greek story *The Iliad*, a chimaera is described as "a thing of immortal make, not human ... lion-fronted and snake behind, a goat in the middle and snorting out the breath of the terrible flame of bright fire."

● Instead of scales, chimaera have mini "teeth" that cover their skin. Like teeth, these dermal denticles have a central pulp cavity. This is surrounded by a layer of dentine and topped with an enamel-like substance.

● Cartilaginous fish such as rays, sharks, and chimaeras all have dermal denticles on their skin. This makes it very rough to the touch and hard-wearing.

● These odd creatures are known by many different common names, including ghost shark, rat fish, rabbit fish, and spook fish.

Where in the world?

This large group of fish is found in rivers, estuaries, and seas throughout the temperate and cooler waters, although plownoses are found only in the southern hemisphere.

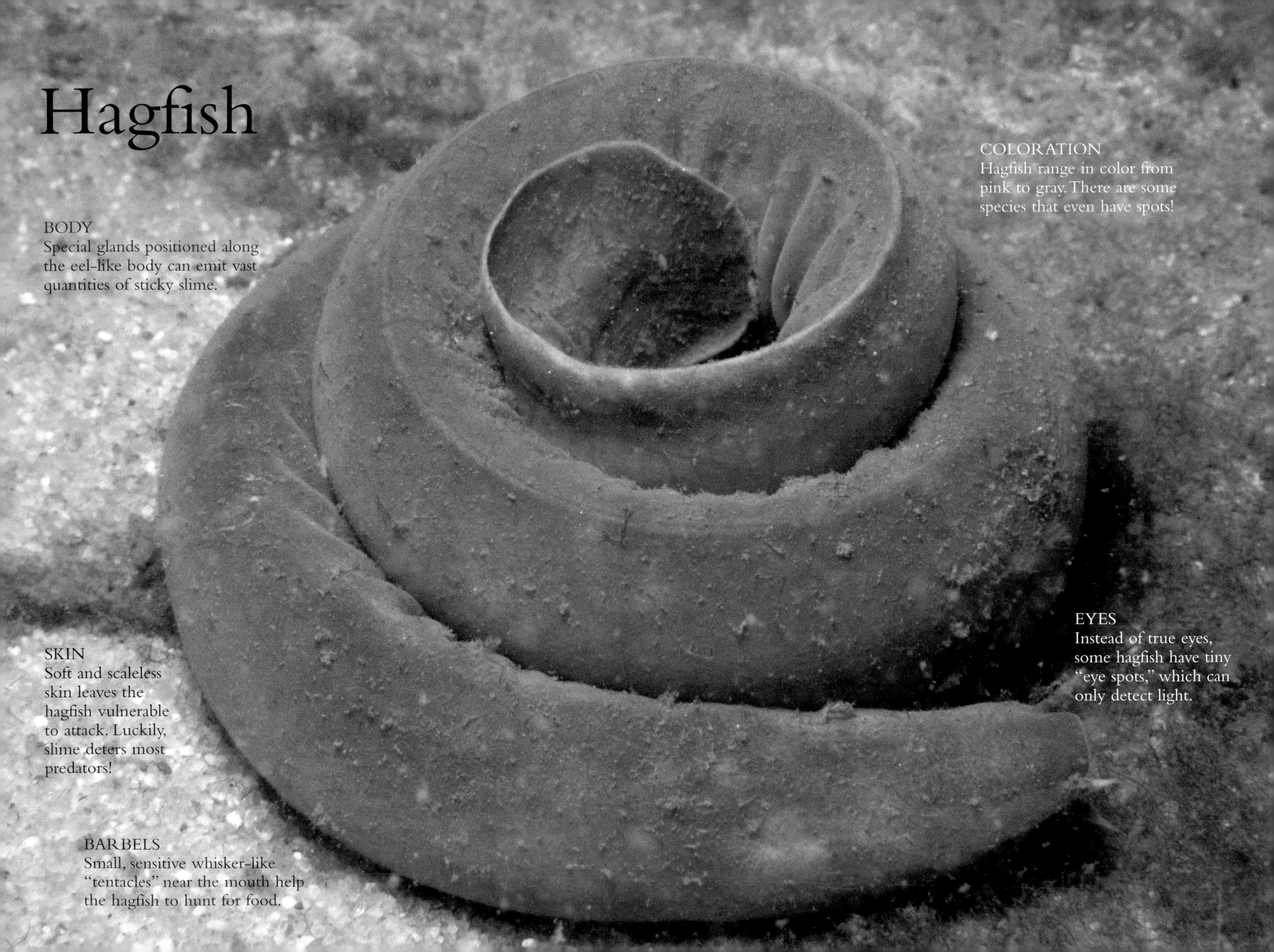

Hagfish

BODY
Special glands positioned along the eel-like body can emit vast quantities of sticky slime.

COLORATION
Hagfish range in color from pink to gray. There are some species that even have spots!

SKIN
Soft and scaleless skin leaves the hagfish vulnerable to attack. Luckily, slime deters most predators!

EYES
Instead of true eyes, some hagfish have tiny "eye spots," which can only detect light.

BARBELS
Small, sensitive whisker-like "tentacles" near the mouth help the hagfish to hunt for food.

These unappealingly ugly fish are justly famous for the huge quantities of mucus they secrete, earning them the nickname "slime eels"! Despite the fact that they have no eyes, no stomach, and no jaws, they are still voracious eaters. It's their superb senses of taste and smell that help them to track down carrion, but they are quite capable of tackling live prey, too. Inside its round mouth is a long, rasping tongue, which cuts into flesh with mechanical efficiency. Having punched a hole in their victim's body, they worm their way in and begin to tear at meat and muscle—consuming their victim from the inside out.

SIZE

Where in the world?

Hagfish have been found in the Asian, Indian, and Pacific oceans. They prefer cool waters and soft sea bottoms, where they can quickly bury themselves to escape from danger.

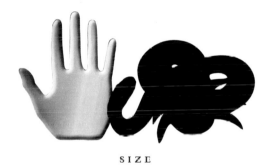

1. WHEN TROUBLE STRIKES, hagfish know how to make the most out of a sticky situation! These slippery creatures secrete a "super slime" that, in contact with water, expands into a gelatinous goo that coats everything it touches. The hagfish has its own trick for escaping this cocoon of slime. It ties itself in a knot and then shuffles the knot down its body to wipe the slime away!

2. THIS BREAM ISN'T SO LUCKY. Its gills are clogged with goo and it soon suffocates. The hagfish isn't about to ignore such a temptingly tasty morsel. It quickly moves in to devour the unsuccessful hunter before other predators get the scent!

Did you know?

● Hagfish have such slow metabolisms that they have been known to survive for up to seven months without eating. This has made them a very adaptable and successful species—able to survive in environments where other fish struggle.

● These primitive creatures are very unusual in that, although they have a partial skull, they have no vertebrae (backbone), which means they cannot be classified as vertebrates.

● Hagfish have a very curious circulatory system that contains four primitive "hearts." One (the brachial heart) acts like the main pump, while the other three are auxiliaries.

● Some species of hagfish are hermaphrodites, meaning that they are born with both male and female sex organs. They change to either male or female as they grow to adulthood.

Manta Ray

PECTORAL FINS
These graceful rays swim by flapping their long pectoral fins as though they were wings.

MOUTH
This type of broad mouth, at the end of the head, is called a terminal.

TEETH
Mantas have about 300 row of tiny teeth. These are not used for feeding.

BODY
The largest manta disk measured 30 ft. (9.1 m) across. The average is 22 ft. (6.7 m).

CEPHALIC FINS
A pair of cephalic fins (or lobes) helps direct and scoop water into the mouth.

With their superbly sculpted bodies and sickle-shaped (falcate) "wings," these magnificent mantas are one of the ocean's most beautiful inhabitants. Despite their great size, they are gentle creatures and present no danger to other ocean-dwellers unless threatened. They're primarily plankton feeders and use their flexible cephalic fins to help scoop up food. This habit has earned them the unflattering nickname "devil ray" because, at rest, these fins look like horns! Although they were once aggressively hunted, mantas and humans now enjoy a much healthier relationship. A large tourist industry has grown up around the appreciation of these wondrous animals, who seem to be as curious about us as we are about them.

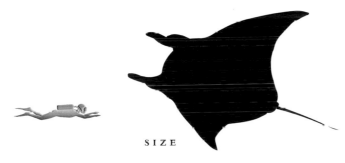

SIZE

MANTAS ARE OVOVIVIPAROUS. Their unborn young start life wrapped in a thin shell, which hatches inside the mother. A few months later, the pups (usually one or two) are born, rolled up like tubes inside their own pectoral fins! These impressive animals start life with disks about 3.9 ft. (1.2 m) across, but they grow rapidly, doubling their size within the first year of life.

Did you know?

● Mantas are descended from stingrays (suborder Myliobatoidei). They therefore share the same flattened body shape, which helps the stingrays to stay hidden on the ocean bottom. They don't, however, have the infamous barbed sting.

● Mantas are amazing acrobats. They can swim at great speed, and juveniles have sometimes been seen to leap clear out of the water. No one knows why, but perhaps it's just for fun!

● Rays are known to be very intelligent; manta rays have the largest brain-to-body ratio of all of the sharks and rays.

● In 2008, people were stunned to discover a manta ray on a sidewalk in San Francisco, California, USA. It's still not known how it got there!

Where in the world?

Giant mantas are circumtropical and inhabit the warm waters of the world's oceans. They are found in both shallow and deep waters, most often around coastlines and rocky reefs.

Sea Lamprey

DORSAL FIN
Two elongated dorsal (back) fins add stability and help the sea lamprey make sudden turns.

BODY
The lamprey's eel-like body can grow up to 3 ft. 11 in. (1.2 m) long.

GILL PORES
Seven round gill openings are positioned on either side of the sea lamprey's head.

ORAL DISK
Instead of a mouth is a wide disk, filled with tiny teeth arranged in circular rows.

EYES
It's only when lampreys reach adulthood (after about seven years) that their eyes develop fully.

These primitive parasites love just one thing: the taste of fresh blood! Inside their tubular mouths are razor-sharp teeth, arranged in circular rows, which work like a can opener. By boring a hole in their victim's flesh, the lamprey is able to expose the raw and bloody muscle beneath. An anticoagulant in its saliva keeps the wound open and prevents the blood from clotting until the lamprey has eaten its fill. Lamprey larvae are harmless, but once these eel-like leaches reach adulthood, they become real pests. They prey on a wide range of species, including sharks and whales, and have had a serious impact on fish populations where they have been accidentally introduced.

SIZE

Where in the world?

This successful species is found in the Mediterranean and North Atlantic. It is also found in the Great Lakes where, in the past, it has decimated local fish populations.

1. ADULT LAMPREYS are real-life blood-suckers, and this one has just spotted a new "donor"! Swimming up to the fast-moving fish, it wastes no time. Attaching its sucker-like mouth to the fish's scaly skin, it punches a hole through its victim's flank.

2. IN A MATTER OF MOMENTS, the lamprey is feeding. Like a leach, it gorges on its victim's blood and releases its grip only when it is no longer hungry.

3. THE TROUT IS DAZED and weak from blood loss. The ocean is a harsh environment to survive in and, in this state, it's unlikely to live. By then, the lamprey will have moved on to fresh feeding grounds.

Did you know?

● Sea lamprey are an anadromous species. Just like salmon (family Salmonidae), they spend most of their lives at sea but return to freshwater lakes and streams to spawn.

● Lamprey larvae, called ammocoetes, spend their first five years buried in the mud or sand at the bottom of freshwater lakes and streams.

● Unlike adults, lamprey ammocoetes feed by filtering small particles of food from the water. It's only once they are fully grown that they develop that vicious, sucker-like mouth.

● Adult lampreys live in the oceans, but when they are ready to spawn, they return to the lake or stream in which they were born. Spawning adults are unable to eat, and after they have laid and fertilized their eggs, they die.

Barracuda

COLORATION
Colors vary between species. Most are dark greenish-blue or gray on their upper body.

EYES
A pair of large eyes enables the barracuda to spot prey even when visibility is poor.

TAIL
It takes a lot of energy to swim, so this wide tail helps give the barracuda "thrust."

BODY
A streamlined shape helps reduce "resistance" as the barracuda pushes its body through the water.

SCALES
Small, smooth scales cover the body. These protect the fish and grow as the barracuda grows.

Powering through the oceans like a meat-seeking missile, the barracuda is a fearsome sight. Some species grow up to 5 ft. 11 in. (1.8 m) in length and almost 12 in. (30 cm) in width. The barracuda's body is streamlined, which allows it to reach speeds of up to 27 mph (43 km/h) in pursuit of prey. Its large eyes give it excellent vision when hunting in murky waters, while its elongated jaw is full of fang-like teeth for gripping and tearing at flesh. This killer combination makes the barracuda one of the top reef predators, able to feed on a wide variety of fish and squid.

SIZE

DESPITE DIFFERENCES IN SIZE AND COLOR between the estimated 27 barracuda species, they all have an elongated body, powerful jaws, and a large swim bladder. While their thin, flexible bodies are well adapted for racing through coral reefs, it's the large swim bladder that gives them a real advantage. This is because it enables them to change buoyancy—to rise and sink—very quickly when chasing prey.

Where in the world?

These handsome hunters live in tropical and subtropical seas. They are most commonly found in the shallower waters around coral reefs. Juveniles may even enter river estuaries and mangrove swamps.

Did you know?

● Adult barracudas are usually solitary hunters. Younger fish, though, will often gather together in large groups. The collective name for such a group of barracudas is a battery.

● Barracudas, like magpies, are said to be attracted to shiny, reflective objects such as gold necklaces or diamond earrings. This may be because they shimmer in the same way as fish scales. Divers are advised not to wear jewelry when they swim near barracuda territory, in case they attract unwanted attention!

● The great barracuda (*Sphyraena barracuda*) is such a powerful predator that it has been nicknamed the "tiger of the sea."

● Why change a winning formula? Barracudas have barely changed since their ancestors first appeared on Earth 50 million years ago.

Toadfish

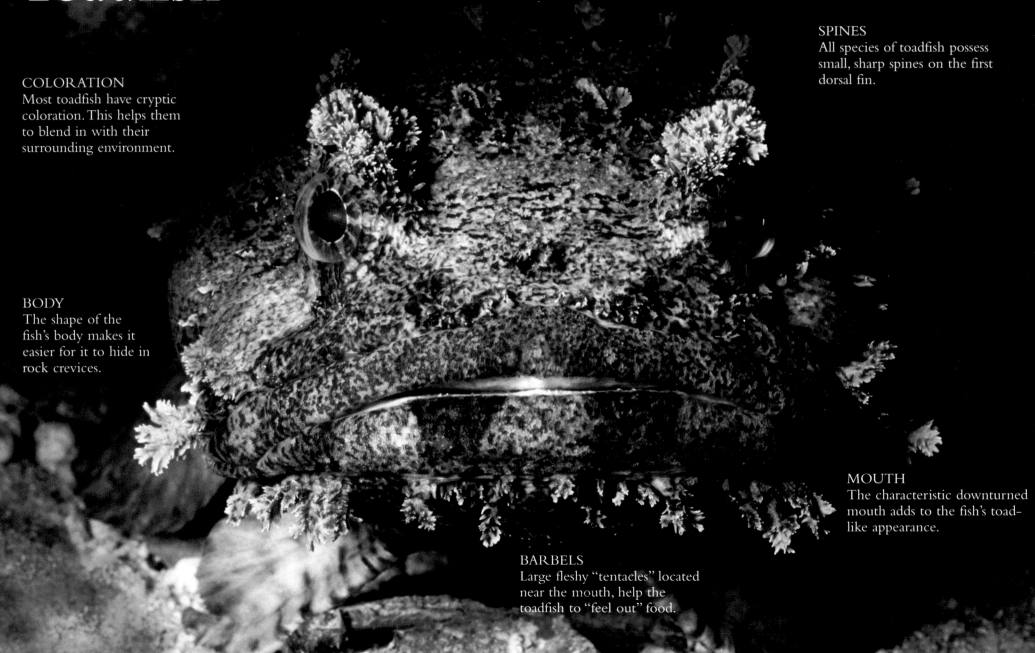

SPINES
All species of toadfish possess small, sharp spines on the first dorsal fin.

COLORATION
Most toadfish have cryptic coloration. This helps them to blend in with their surrounding environment.

BODY
The shape of the fish's body makes it easier for it to hide in rock crevices.

MOUTH
The characteristic downturned mouth adds to the fish's toad-like appearance.

BARBELS
Large fleshy "tentacles" located near the mouth, help the toadfish to "feel out" food.

It's easy to see why these flat-featured critters are known as toadfish. With their wide mouths, big heads, bulbous eyes, and smooth, shiny skin, they do indeed look like toads. But that's where the resemblance ends. These funny-looking fish are actually skilled ambush hunters, feeding on sea worms, crustaceans, mollusks, and other fish. They often hide in rock crevices or dig dens in the sandy sea bed, where they wait for a snack to swim by. Their flattened shape and cryptic camouflage are ideal for staying hidden in rocky crevices, while upturned eyes and rows of fleshy barbels around that wide mouth help them find food in the murky depths.

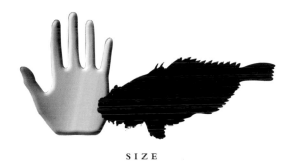

SIZE

Where in the world?

Toadfish make their homes on sandy and muddy marine bottoms. Species are found from the Americas to Australasia, but members of the subfamily Thlassophryininae inhabit the Eastern Pacific and Western Atlantic.

1. REACHING INTO HIS LOBSTER pot to check out the previous evening's catch, this fisherman is blissfully unaware that danger lurks just beneath his fingertips. Toadfish can survive for up to 24 hours out of water and, hidden in the cool, damp sand inside the pot, a nasty surprise is waiting.

2. MEMBERS OF THE SUBFAMILY Thlassophryininae are poisonous. Those small spines on the toadfish's back may look relatively harmless, but each one is hollow and connected to a gland that is loaded with venom. The poison is potent enough to cause an extremely painful wound and, if it's not treated quickly, infection could set in.

Did you know?

● In the mating season, male toadfish "sing"—although not very tunefully! The distinctive hum is made by releasing air from their swim bladder. It's so loud that it can easily be heard above the surface of the water!

● It's believed that the toadfish uses his "song" to attract females to his nest. Each male builds his own nest in the muddy sea bed and interested females come along to deposit their eggs.

● Presumably, the more accomplished "singers" attract more mates, but usually most nests contain the eggs of several different females.

● The male diligently guards the eggs until they hatch and for at least four weeks after—until the young are big and strong enough to look after themselves.

Stingray

STING
Most stingrays have one or more barbed stings on their tail. These are used for self-defense.

BODY
FAMILY UROLOPHIDAE
Members of the family Urolophidae are also known as round stingrays due to their disk shape.

BODY
FAMILY DASYATIDAE
Members of this group have disks that range from oval to diamond-like in shape.

TAIL
FAMILY UROLOPHIDAE
Round stingrays have a slender tail, which is generally shorter than their disk.

TAIL
FAMILY DASYATIDAE
This family is also known as whiptails. Their tails are much longer than their disks.

The sight of a stingray skimming across the sea floor is one of the ocean's great spectacles. These beautiful creatures move more like birds than fish, using their flattened pectoral fins to flap through the shallows with amazing agility. There are eight families within the stingray order and they are recognized for their intelligence and gentleness. Most are found in warm coastal waters, but there are also deep-sea and river species. Although they vary in shape, color, and size, all have one or more poisonous spines, which give the group its common name. These spines can kill, but rays only sting reflexively, throwing up their barbed tail to ward off any threat.

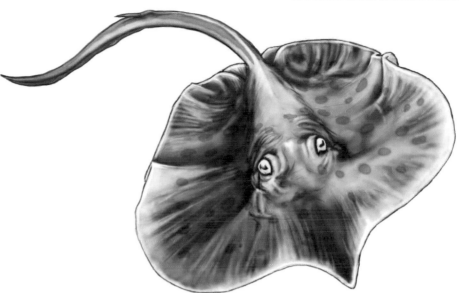

THIS FLATTENED BODY SHAPE IS IDEAL FOR FISH, like the stingray, that spend much of their time concealed under sand on the sea bed. Their eyes are on top of their body so that they can still see prey while hidden. However, they also have special sensing organs under the skin (ampullae of Lorenzini), which enable them to detect the electromagnetic fields emitted by living animals.

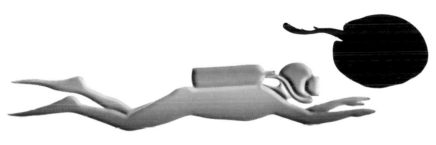

SIZE

Did you know?

• Millions of years ago, the ray's pectoral fins evolved into the disk-like wings that make this species so distinctive.

• Some species of stingray have powerful "plates" inside their mouths, which they use for crushing the shells of their favorite foods—mollusks and crustaceans.

• Like sharks, stingrays are cartilaginous fish. They have skeletons that are made of cartilage (a flexible connective tissue usually found between bones) rather than actual bone.

• One of the most popular venues for divers is Stingray City, in the Caribbean. Here, it is possible to swim with the local, southern stingrays (*Dasyatis americana*) with little danger, as long as divers respect the rays.

Where in the world?

Stingrays are common in warm coastal waters throughout the world's oceans. Deep-sea, temperate, and freshwater species are also known, but most inhabit the rich feeding grounds around reefs.

Freshwater Fish

Less than three percent of the planet's water is freshwater, yet this rare resource is home to many species. Some migrate from one environment to another—living at sea, but returning to the rivers where they were born, to spawn. Other species live only in freshwater and have evolved accordingly. Peters' elephantnose fish (*Gnathonemus petersii*) has a long snout for rooting out food in muddy river beds. And the alligator gar (*Atractosteus spatula*) breathes air, enabling it to thrive in the shallowest of swamps.

Piranhas are well-known freshwater fish. They are often regarded as dangerous, but although they can be aggressive during the breeding season, their reputation is not entirely deserved.

Alligator Gar

COLORATION
The upper (dorsal) surface of this fish's long, muscular body is dark brown to olive-green in color.

SCALES
Overlapping, protective bony scales, known as scutes, cover the body and make impressive armor.

BODY
A streamlined shape helps reduce resistance as the gar pushes its body through the water.

HEAD
The gar's common name comes from its long teeth and its alligator-like, elongated snout.

SWIM BLADDER
This functions like a primitive lung, enabling the gar to breathe air in shallow water.

If we could go back to the Cretaceous Period, 145 million years ago, we would find living alongside the dinosaurs the ancestors of the alligator gar. Today, these powerful predators still impress. It's their distinctive alligator-style snout that gives these huge hunters their common name. Although they are increasingly rare, these superb fish have survived so long because they have a winning "design": their bodies are streamlined for speed and are covered in protective bony scales. Their big eyes are able to pinpoint prey with great efficiency. Like all fish, they have gills, but their swim bladder also functions like a primitive lung, so that it can gulp air when water levels fall in the summer.

SIZE

Where in the world?

These predators can be found in pools, rivers, and swamps and along the gulf-coast region of Mexico and the USA—from Florida to Veracruz. They are mainly found in the Mississippi basin.

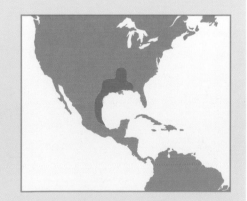

1. BASKING IN THE SLOW-MOVING waters of the bayou, the gar is almost invisible thanks to its natural coloration, which blends in with the leaf-logged waters. However, when a young alligator crosses its path, it throws caution—and camouflage—to the wind! Surging forward with a sudden rush of speed, the 'gator is taken completely by surprise.

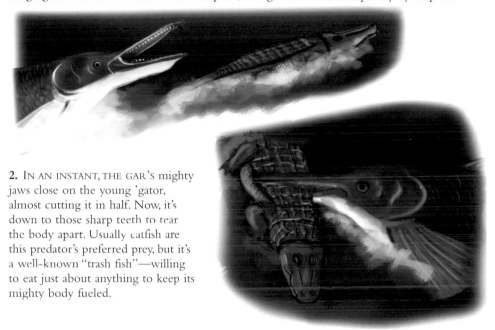

2. IN AN INSTANT, THE GAR'S mighty jaws close on the young 'gator, almost cutting it in half. Now, it's down to those sharp teeth to tear the body apart. Usually catfish are this predator's preferred prey, but it's a well-known "trash fish"—willing to eat just about anything to keep its mighty body fueled.

Did you know?

● There are seven known species of gar. These are found mainly in freshwater rivers and lakes, although some are known to venture out as far as the brackish waters around coastal estuaries.

● The alligator gar's eggs are extremely poisonous. Predators have learnt to avoid them, so most of their young survive to adulthood.

● The gar's armor-plating is said to be so tough that it can produce sparks when struck by an ax!

● The gar gets its name from an Old English word meaning "spear." This is especially appropriate because its bony scales were once used by native Americans to make spear and arrow heads. Today, their fearsome appearance makes them a popular sports fish.

Sturgeon

SCUTES
Instead of scales, rows of protective, bony plates called scutes run along the fish's flank.

BODY
The elongated body has no scales, a large tail fin, and a pointed, beak-like snout.

MOUTH
Sturgeon have no teeth, but can form their mouths into a tube to suck in food.

BARBELS
Sensitive barbels help the sturgeon to detect food in the muddy waters where visibility is low.

COLORING
These freshwater giants have a greenish-gray coloring, which helps them blend in with their surroundings.

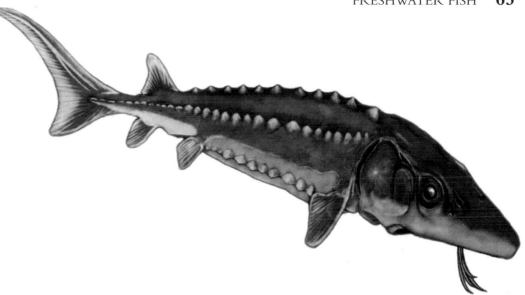

These extraordinary fish breed in the chilly waters of North America and Northern Europe. There, they make a surprisingly good living, scouring the river beds for plants and animals, which they suck up into their tube-like mouths. Some species, such as the mighty beluga (*Huso huso*) may grow up to 18 ft. long (5.5 m) and weigh as much as 4,400 lb. (1,996 kg). However, it takes a long time for a fish to grow this big—at least 20 years—so they are very vulnerable to overfishing and pollution. This has caused massive drops in sturgeon populations in recent years. Thankfully, efforts are being made to save this superb species for future generations to enjoy.

SIZE

Where in the world?

This widespread species is most at home in the cool waters of Northern seas, rivers, and lakes. Some species are entirely freshwater, but a few venture into the open oceans.

THERE ARE AT LEAST 26 KNOWN SPECIES OF STURGEON. These vary in size from giants like the kaluga (*Huso dauricus*) to relative tiddlers such as the sterlet (*Acipenser ruthenus*). Using its tube-like mouth, the biggest sturgeon can suck up fish as large as salmon. Smaller species use their wedge-shaped snouts to root through the muddy river bed, where they find invertebrates, crustaceans, and insect larvae.

Did you know?

● Several species of sturgeon are harvested for their roe (eggs), which is made into caviar. This luxury food sells for a small fortune in some parts of the world, making sturgeon the most valuable—pound for pound—of all fish.

● Freshwater sturgeon can live for an extremely long time. One, caught in Canada in 1953, was estimated to be 152 years old. Today, most live for only a few decades.

● Freshwater sturgeon, like salmon (family Salmonidae), return each spring to spawn in the streams and rivers where they were born.

● Between 1879 and 1900, the fishermen around the Great Lakes caught an average of 3,968 lb. (1.8 metric tons) of sturgeon a year!

Peters' Elephantnose Fish

EYES
Elephantnose fish have poor eyesight. Luckily, they do not rely on their vision to catch prey.

BODY
The body is flattened (laterally compressed) and a dark brown to black in color.

NOSE
This elephantnose isn't really a nose at all, but the fish's massively elongated jaw.

MOUTH
A tiny mouth is filled with small, pointed teeth—ideal for gripping slippery fish!

ELECTRORECEPTORS
Electroreceptors in the nose and along much of the fish's body help it hunt and navigate.

These remarkable fish are quite at home in the dark, slow-flowing water of Africa's Niger and Congo river basins, thanks to some very special adaptations. Elephantnoses are mormyrids—"electric fish." They navigate and hunt by generating and detecting electrical signals. Their "generator" is located in the thinnest part of the tail and produces rapid pulses of electricity. This creates a field around the fish's body. Electroreceptors along the head and upper and lower body monitor changes to the field as well as detecting other fields. This enables the elephantnose to build up a picture of the world around it, no matter how dark and murky the surrounding water is.

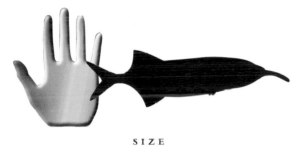

SIZE

Where in the world?

Peters' elephantnose fish are found in Africa's Niger and Congo river basins. They spend much of their time amid the mud and vegetation on the river bed, where they can hunt for food undetected.

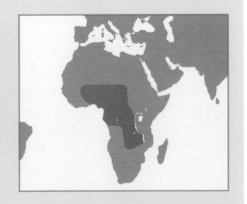

1. THIS FEISTY FISH has a sense of hearing that is supplemented by an organ called the lateral line (a), which detects vibrations in the water. In many species, the position of the lateral line can be seen as a physical line along each side of the fish's body.

2. ELECTRORECEPTORS (b) in the skin detect changes in electrical fields caused by nearby objects. Chemical sensors (c) in the jaw pick up "scents" carried by the water. Finally, hollow tubes connect bony plates in the skull to the ear (d), which gives the elephantnose a fine sense of hearing.

Did you know?

● Most fish have small brains in comparison to their overall body weight. Some are very small indeed. For instance, the pike (family Esocidae) has a brain that makes up just 0.08 percent of its entire body mass. The brain of the elephantnose accounts for 3.1 percent of its body weight.

● This means that if the elephantnose grew to the same size as the pike, its brain would be 40 times larger.

● We humans have, on average, a brain that weighs in at around 2.3 percent of our body weight. That doesn't mean that elephantnoses are smarter than us—it's not just size that is important, but also the complexity of the brain.

● Elephantnoses are a very curious, intelligent, and playful species.

Tiger Fish

COLORATION
Most species have one or more dark stripes along their body. Goliaths have no stripes.

EYES
A pair of large eyes helps the tiger fish to track and catch its prey.

BODY
The muscular body is streamlined, which reduces drag as the fish pushes through the water.

TEETH
Interlocking teeth work like scissors to slice chunks of flesh off the body of its prey.

SIZE
The largest tiger fish is the goliath, which can grow 6 ft. (1.8 m) long.

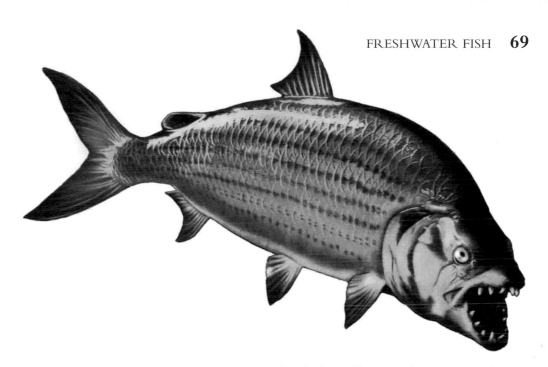

Tiger fish are one of the African continent's most notorious freshwater species—and there's no doubt that they deserve their evocative nickname. These fish are fast, powerful predators that hunt in packs, using their sleek, muscular bodies to run down prey. They are most often found in fast-flowing rivers, where they can easily outpace less powerful fish that may struggle to swim against the pull of the current. A school of hungry young tiger fish will attack almost anything that crosses its path. However, even a lone adult will tackle a fish as large as itself. If food is scarce, tiger fish have even been known to turn cannibal!

TIGER FISH HAVE AN AIR-FILLED sac in their body, which acts like a sound receiver. It picks up vibrations from the water, enabling them to home in on nearby animals. Tigers are famously aggressive, and larger species will tackle almost anything, including animals that stray too close to the water's edge! Most hunt in small groups, but they are equally happy to hunt solo.

SIZE

Where in the world?

Members of the genus *Hydrocynus* are endemic to Africa, meaning that they are found nowhere else. They prefer fast-flowing waters, where they have an advantage over less powerful fish.

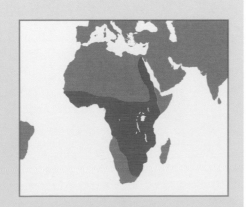

Did you know?

● "Tiger" is a popular common name for many species of predatory fish. This colorful moniker has been given to fish from four different family groups inhabiting three different continents (Africa, Asia, and South America).

● The largest member of the genus *Hydrocynus,* the goliath (*Hydrocynus goliath*) is also the most famous, thanks to its fearsome appearance. These big beasts are mainly found in the Congo River Basin, Lakes Tanganyika and Upemba, and the Lualaba River.

● Strangely, the species name for these tigers actually translates as "water dog"—from *hydro,* meaning "water" and *kyon,* meaning "dog."

● These strong, streamlined predators gave their name to the Mark 24 Tigerfish torpedo, which was famously used by the British Royal Navy for many years.

Sawfish

SAW
The saw, or rostrum, as it is also called, typically has 14 to 22 "teeth" on each side.

SPIRACLES
Spiracles behind the eye enable the sawfish to breathe while lying buried in the mud.

BODY
A flattened body enables sawfish to spend much of their time lying on the river bed.

MOUTH
The mouth is on the underside of the fish's body and is lined with tiny teeth.

GILLS
Sawfish are a type of ray and have gills on the underside of their bodies.

With its flattened body, slender tail, and massive "saw," these odd fish look like something put together from spare parts. The reason for the strange shape is that sawfish are related to rays and have the flattened body of a bottom-dwelling species. That strange-looking saw, too, is much more practical than it seems. It can be used in self-defense, but it is at its most effective in finding food. By simply swiping its saw from side to side, sawfish can stun or impale small fish with ease. The saw is also packed with sensors that enable it to detect the slightest movement under the mud and so add crustaceans and invertebrates to the menu!

SIZE

Where in the world?

Being able to travel between brackish and freshwater, sawfish are usually found in coastal waters and rivers. The largest freshwater populations are in Australia, New Guinea, and Lake Nicaragua.

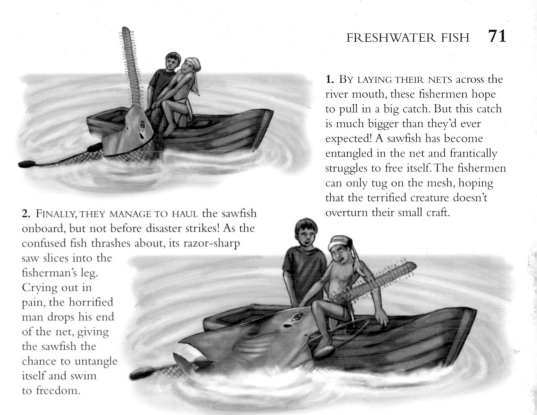

1. BY LAYING THEIR NETS across the river mouth, these fishermen hope to pull in a big catch. But this catch is much bigger than they'd ever expected! A sawfish has become entangled in the net and frantically struggles to free itself. The fishermen can only tug on the mesh, hoping that the terrified creature doesn't overturn their small craft.

2. FINALLY, THEY MANAGE TO HAUL the sawfish onboard, but not before disaster strikes! As the confused fish thrashes about, its razor-sharp saw slices into the fisherman's leg. Crying out in pain, the horrified man drops his end of the net, giving the sawfish the chance to untangle itself and swim to freedom.

Did you know?

● Most fish have bodies that are adapted to survive in either salt- or freshwater. This saw-snouted species is unusual in that it is able to travel between salt- and freshwater.

● Some sawfish inhabit warm tropical coastal waters, around bays and estuaries. Some are freshwater specialists. The largetooth sawfish (*Pristis microdon*) is most often found in rivers in Australia, New Guinea, Indonesia, and Nigeria. Freshwater sawfish have also been found as far afield as Britain!

● This preference for estuaries and rivers has made sawfish extremely vulnerable to pollution and overfishing and most species are now endangered.

● The green sawfish (*Pristis zijsron*) is the largest species, growing to 24 ft. (7.3 m) in length—longer than the biggest known great white shark (*Carcharodon carcharias*).

Piranha

HEAD
Piranha have a characteristically flattened face with a large, projecting lower jaw and downturned mouth.

EYES
Large eyes face slightly forward, which helps the piranha to judge distances more accurately.

NOSTRILS
Large nasal pits on top of the head enable piranhas to "taste" the water for food.

BODY
The body is short and flat, with a long, muscular tail for powering through the water.

TEETH
Piranha have interlocking teeth that work like scissors to slice chunks of flesh off the body of their prey.

In his book *Through the Brazilian Wilderness,* the U.S. president Theodore Roosevelt (1858-1919) depicted piranha as terrifying creatures. "They are one of the most ferocious fish in the world ... they mutilate swimmers ... they ... rend and devour alive any wounded man or beast; for blood in the water excites them to madness." Yet, Roosevelt's observations were based on piranha that had been corraled and trapped to provide him with a spectacular show. Naturally, they are lone predators and recent research has suggested that they shoal more for protection than to hunt. They can be aggressive during the breeding season, but like sharks, their bad reputation is not entirely deserved.

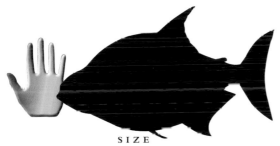

SIZE

A PIRANHA'S TEETH ARE ITS MOST distinctive feature. They are relatively small, but incredibly sharp and interlocking. So, when a piranha closes its overlapping jaws, these razor-sharp wedges snap together, slicing off circular chunks of flesh. Bite marks like this are often seen on the fins and tails of Amazonian fish. Despite this, not all piranha are meat-eaters. Some eat fruit that falls into the river.

Did you know?

● The piranha's "bad boy" image has been exploited by filmmakers for decades. In fact, there have been three movies called *Piranha.* Even now that we know more about these much maligned fish, most people prefer the myth to the reality!

● Piranha have been found in parts of the USA and Bangladesh. It's believed that they may have been released from aquariums.

● Many people who keep these fish are disappointed to discover that even the notorious red-bellied piranha (*Pygocentrus nattereri*) is surprisingly timid and spends much of its time hiding under foliage at the bottom of the tank!

● Male piranhas guard their eggs and fry until they are mature. It is when males are protecting their young that attacks on people are most likely.

Where in the world?

Naturally Piranha are found in the rivers and lakes of tropical South America. They are found in the Amazon basin, in the Orinoco, Paraná, and São Francisco rivers.

Jellyfish, Octopus, and Squid

Perhaps the most bizarre of all sea creatures are the jellies and the cephalopods (squid and octopus). There are around 800 species of cephalopod and at least 2,000 types of jellyfish. These invertebrates can be found in every ocean, from the deepest, darkest waters to the shallowest shores. Some jellyfish have even been found in freshwater. Species like the lion's mane jellyfish (*Cyanea capillata*) or the giant squid (genus *Architeuthis*) can grow to incredible sizes—some as large as a whale.

Jellyfish and cephalopods are extraordinarily complex. Scientists are only just beginning to understand the lifestyle and behavior of these strange creatures, as well as how their bodies function.

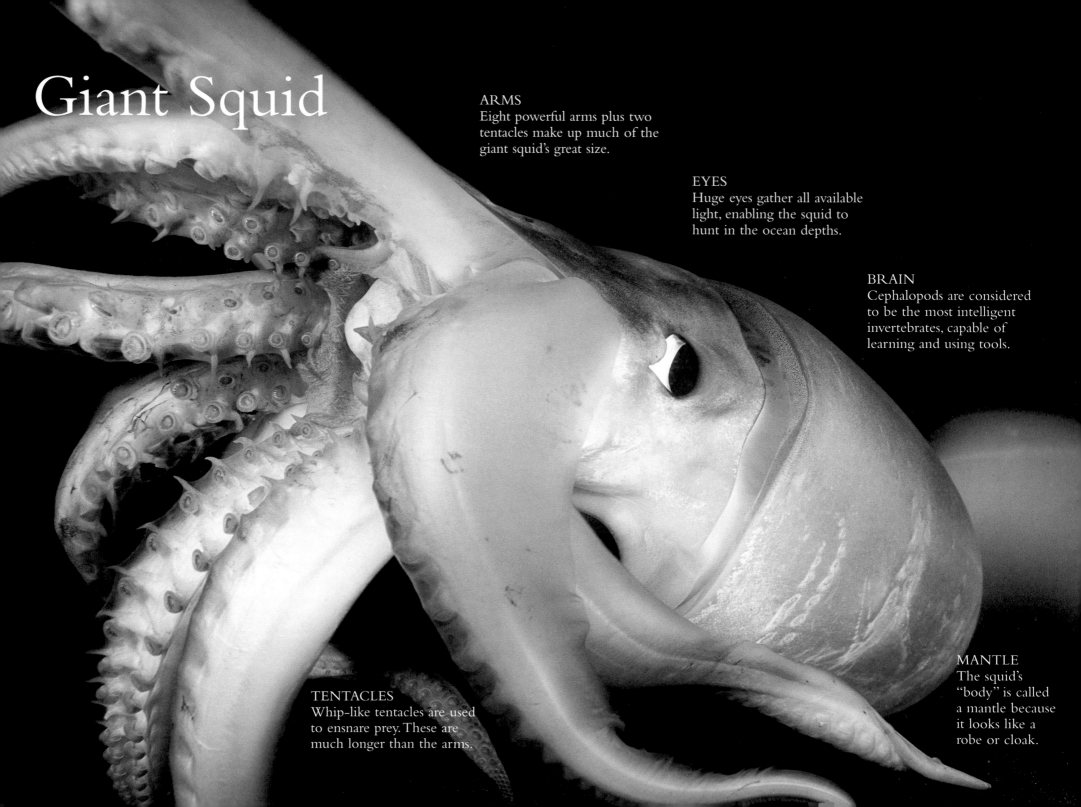

Giant Squid

ARMS
Eight powerful arms plus two
tentacles make up much of the
giant squid's great size.

EYES
Huge eyes gather all available
light, enabling the squid to
hunt in the ocean depths.

BRAIN
Cephalopods are considered
to be the most intelligent
invertebrates, capable of
learning and using tools.

TENTACLES
Whip-like tentacles are used
to ensnare prey. These are
much longer than the arms.

MANTLE
The squid's
"body" is called
a mantle because
it looks like a
robe or cloak.

Imagine a creature that can grow to at least 43 ft. (13 m) long, has eight arms, and two even longer tentacles. These arms are incredibly dextrous and are used to hold and manipulate objects. The tentacles are used solely for feeding, and are tipped with huge suckers to grip onto prey. Now, imagine that the same creature has eyes as big as dinner plates and a sharp, parrot-like beak. Next, add a "jet-propelled" body that moves by pushing water through a fleshy, mantle cavity. Finally, give the creature the ability to communicate with others of its species using color-changing organs in the skin. The result is the giant squid.

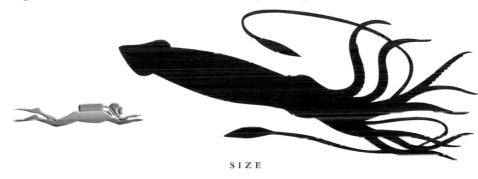

SIZE

Where in the world?

Giant squid are found in the world's oceans. There is little accurate data about these great creatures, but the fact that they are often pulled up in trawler nets suggests that they prefer deeper waters.

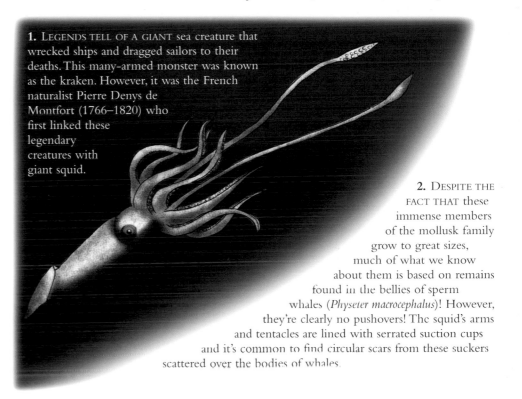

1. LEGENDS TELL OF A GIANT sea creature that wrecked ships and dragged sailors to their deaths. This many-armed monster was known as the kraken. However, it was the French naturalist Pierre Denys de Montfort (1766–1820) who first linked these legendary creatures with giant squid.

2. DESPITE THE FACT THAT these immense members of the mollusk family grow to great sizes, much of what we know about them is based on remains found in the bellies of sperm whales (*Physeter macrocephalus*)! However, they're clearly no pushovers! The squid's arms and tentacles are lined with serrated suction cups and it's common to find circular scars from these suckers scattered over the bodies of whales.

Did you know?

● The only living creature with eyes larger than the giant squid is its relative, the colossal squid (*Mesonychoteuthis hamiltoni*).

● Giant squid have a balance organ called a statocyst. This sac contains sensory hairs, known as setae, which react to changes in direction, orientation, and speed. This lets the squid know which way up it is!

● These giants are very elusive. The first photographs of a live giant squid in its natural environment were taken only in 2004. The National Science Museum of Japan and the Ogasawara Whale Watching Association took nearly two years to accomplish this scientific first.

● Inside the statocyst is a mineral called the statolith. Growth rings, similar to the rings inside a tree, can be used to calculate the squid's age.

Sea Nettle

BELL: SIZE
The bell typically grows to 6–8 in. (2.4-3.1 cm) in diameter, depending on the species.

ARMS
The sea nettle has four oral arms. These help take prey to the mouth.

TENTACLES
This curious creature has tentacles surrounding its mouth, which help it capture food.

BELL: SEMI-TRANSPARENT
Some sea nettles are semi-transparent. Their bells have small, whitish dots and reddish-brown stripes.

BELL: OPAQUE
Some sea nettles have white or opaque bells. These tend not to have dots or stripes.

Jetting through the coastal waters of the Atlantic and Pacific, these umbrella-shaped jellies look like unlikely hunters. Yet, surrounding that delicate bell are at least 20 tentacles, all armed with stinging cells. These inject a chemical cocktail into the jelly's victim, which paralyzes and—ultimately—kills it. The tentacles are often used for defense. Large creatures that get caught in the jellyfish's tentacles can suffer serious damage. But sea nettles are pernicious predators and use their stinging tentacles and oral arms to catch a wide range of prey. Many jellies feed on microscopic plankton, but the sea nettle eats small fish, worms, larvae, and even other jellyfish.

SIZE

Where in the world?

East coast sea nettles (*Chrysaora quinquecirrha*) are found along the North American coastline and in the Atlantic Ocean. West coast species (*Chrysaora fuscescens*) live along the western coastline and the Pacific Ocean.

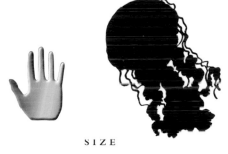

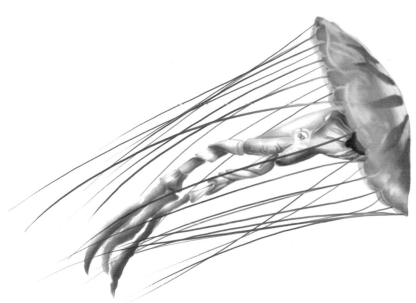

THE SEA NETTLE, like all members of the phylum Cnidaria, has stinging cells on its tentacles, which it uses to capture prey and for self-defense. These bulb-shaped cells, called nematocysts, have a coiled thread inside, which is lined with barbs. When prey comes close, the capsule is triggered, the nematocysts are "fired," and poison is injected into their target. All of this happens in nanoseconds.

Did you know?

● Sea nettle venom is strong enough to kill small fish. Larger fish may be paralyzed by the toxin, which gives the nettle enough time to escape from potential predators.

● Humans who have been stung find that sea nettle venom produces a very painful rash. Stings are not usually fatal, unless the person is repeatedly stung or is allergic to the toxin.

● Jellies don't have brains—at least, not as we know them! Instead, they have a loose network of nerves under the skin, which is known as a nerve net.

● Jellyfish aren't fish at all. To avoid confusion, some scientists call them (and other soft-bodied sea-dwellers) gelatinous zooplankton.

North Pacific Giant Octopus

CHROMATOPHORES
If danger strikes, special cells in the skin help the octopus blend with its surroundings.

BODY
These amazing animals are invertebrates, which means that their soft body has no internal skeleton.

ARMS
Octopi have four pairs of arms that measure, on average, 16 ft. 1 in. (4.9 m) in length.

MOUTH
Octopi love crustaceans and they use their tough beak-like mouths to crush up shells.

SUCKERS
The arms are lined with suckers. The rims of these suckers are particularly sensitive.

Despite having no skeleton, no protective scales, and no jaws, these giant cephalopods have their own ways of staying safe. They can hide in clouds of toxic ink. They can change their color to blend with their surroundings. They can swim out of danger by forcing water through their body cavity to create their very own "jet engine." Or they can simply tackle their assailant head-on. Seals, sea otters, and even sharks have been found bearing battle scars from the powerful arms and razor-sharp "beak" of this mighty marine mollusk. But the North Pacific giant octopus has brains as well as brawn, and is, in fact, one of the most intelligent of all invertebrates.

SIZE

Where in the world?

These giants live off the coast of southern California and along the Pacific North Western coastline, from Alaska as far as the Aleutian Islands and across to Japan.

1. THIS SCENE MAY SEEM alarming, but the diver has little to fear from this giant of the oceans. The octopus uses its flexible arms and sensitive suckers to explore and "taste" the world around it. It is wrapping its arms around this diver from curiosity, not animosity.

2. THE DIVER IS QUICKLY RELEASED and the octopus settles back down on the sea bed to wait for something tastier to cross its path. Crustaceans, mollusks, fish, sharks, and even other octopi are on the menu, but having "sampled" the peculiar taste and texture of a wet suit, this octopus has decided that divers aren't especially appetizing!

Did you know?

● New-born octopi are no bigger than a grain of rice, but by the time that they reach adulthood, these marine giants can measure over 29 ft. 6 in. (9 m) in length.

● Octopi are famous for their ability to release ink. This creates a "smoke screen" to help them escape from danger. Unbelievably, the ink is toxic to the octopus!

● Octopi are problem-solvers and tool-users. In laboratory conditions, they have shown the ability to learn, remember, and solve puzzles by trial and error.

● These cephalopods are devoted mothers. Adult females lay up to 100,000 eggs, which they care for over the course of many weeks. During this time, they don't eat and they die soon after their young hatch.

Nautilus

SHELL
Inside the shell are chambers containing air and seawater. More are added as the nautilus grows.

RADULA
The radula is a little like a "toothy" rough tongue, which mollusks use to grind food.

COLORATION
The spiral shell has two layers. The outer is brown and white. Inside, it's pearly silver.

TENTACLES
Up to 90 small, suckerless tentacles are attached to the body, near the shell opening.

EYES
Despite having large eyes, the nautilus likely has poor vision.

They're not big, powerful, or fast, yet nautiluses have been around for at least 500 million years. Back in the Cambrian Period (542–488 million years ago), these magnificent mollusks were some of the most successful predators in the ancient oceans. Today, only six known species survive, of which the emperor nautilus (*Nautilus pompilius pompilius*) is the largest, growing up to 8 in. (20 cm) long. These beautiful creatures resemble other cephalopods, in that they have a large head and a "foot" that has been modified into tentacles. However, their defining characteristic is that gloriously coiled shell, which the American author Oliver Wendell Holmes (1809-1894) immortalized in verse as a "ship of pearl."

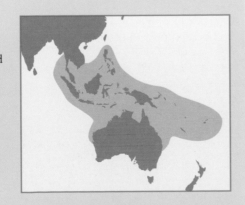

SIZE

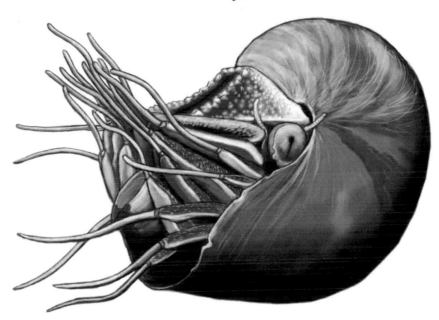

Inside this coiled shell are chambers containing air and seawater, which can be adjusted to change the nautiluses' buoyancy. As they grow, more chambers are added (up to 30), although the mollusk lives in the outermost segment only. The shell is thin and light, but its shape and the air chambers inside make it surprisingly strong—able to resist pressure up to 2,600 ft. (792 m).

Did you know?

● When danger strikes, the nautilus simply retreats inside its shell, using two specially adapted tentacles, called a hood, to cover up the entrance.

● As its vision is poor, the nautilus is thought to rely on its sense of smell to find food. Two tentacles, near the eyes, are covered in sensitive cilia, which may help them to "sniff out" prey.

● Nautiluses first appeared in the fossil record 500 million years ago. Although they haven't changed much since then, their ancient ancestors grew much larger—up to 8.2 ft. (2.5 m) in size.

● Nautiluses have an incredibly powerful grip. Once the creature attaches itself to an object, its tentacles can be literally torn off and it still won't release its vice-like grasp!

Where in the world?

Nautiluses can be found in the Indian and Pacific oceans, from the Philippines to Australia. They prefer the deeper waters around coral reefs, but usually enter shallower waters to spawn.

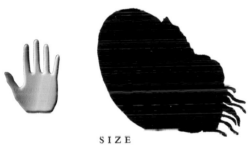

Crustaceans and Mollusks

This is a vast, but poorly understood group. There may be as many as 120,000 species of mollusks and up to 50,000 species of crustaceans. Most make their home in the oceans, but some species thrive in other environments—freshwater rivers, lakes, and even on land. The creatures come in all shapes and sizes, from the almost microscopic *Stygotantulus stocki* to the Japanese spider crab, which is 12 ft. 6 in. (3.8 m) long. One thing unites them all: their armor! Crustaceans and mollusks wear shells.

There are more than 100 species of cuttlefish roaming the seas and oceans of the world. They can blend to match any background, whether it is a sandy sea bed or a rock face.

Cone Shell

TEETH
Venom-filled, radular "teeth" are launched out of the snail's proboscis like miniature harpoons.

SIPHON
Cone shells detect prey using their siphon. This is packed with chemical-detecting sensors called chemoreceptors.

PROBOSCIS
The cone shell's proboscis works like a mouth, engulfing any prey that has been "harpooned."

SHELL
Conus geographus, shown, has one of the more unusual shells; wide and dotted with distinctive spines.

FOOT
Cone shells are gastropods. Gastropod means "stomach foot," because they seem to walk on their bellies.

Crawling along at a snail's pace hasn't prevented the cone shell from becoming a very proficient predator. The secret to its success is hidden inside its tube-like proboscis. There, it carries its very own toxin-laden harpoon, which spears and then paralyzes prey. The toxin is incredibly effective. It needs to be; otherwise any fish harpooned by the cone shell would simply tug itself off its tether and swim away! Ironically, this same venom is now attracting scientific interest because it contains unusual compounds that make it valuable to medical research. So, with interest in this species running high, we could soon know much more about the 4,000 or so members of the complex Coninae group.

SIZE

Where in the world?

Cone shells are indigenous to the coral reefs of the Indo-Pacific. A few species can also be found on the Caribbean coast of the Americas and the Atlantic coast of Africa.

1. IN THE OCEANS, not everything is what it appears to be. This fish, for instance, pays little attention to the cone shell making its slow, steady way along the sea bed. Big mistake!

2. AS IT SWIMS PAST, the cone shell's harpoon shoots out, injecting the unsuspecting fish with powerful paralyzing venom. The harpoon is attached to the sea snail. Once it has hit its target, the fish is actually tethered to its attacker and unable to escape.

3. THE CONE SHELL'S proboscis then expands and slowly, but surely, sucks the fish in—bones, scales, and all! A large meal like this will keep the gastropod well fueled in the days to come.

Did you know?

● In common with most animals, cone shells can be classified by the type of prey they eat. Vermivorus cone shells are worm-eaters, molluscivores are mollusk-eaters, and piscivores are fish-eaters.

● The usual symptoms of cone shell toxin are blurred vision, slurred speech, numbness, and pain. In severe cases, muscle paralysis can lead to death. So far, there is no known anti-toxin.

● Cone shells are a type of sea snail and are related to land-dwelling snails. Both sea snails and their earth-bound cousins belong to the class Gastropoda, which is a very large subgroup within the mollusk family.

● The name "snail" is usually given only to species with an external shell that is big enough for the animal to hide inside. Gastropods without shells are called slugs.

Horseshoe Crab

BODY
The body is divided into three: the head (prosoma), abdomen (opisthosoma), and tail (telson).

PINCERS
Under the head are six pairs of appendages. The pincers pass food to the mouth.

LEGS
Two pairs of jointed legs (pedipalps) are used for walking. The fifth pair is used for pushing forward.

CARAPACE: JUVENILES
As they mature, young horseshoe crabs regularly molt (shed their shell) and grow a new one.

CARAPACE: ADULTS
Full-grown horseshoes don't molt, and their shells often become encrusted with small plants and animals!

Despite its name and its hard outer shell, the horseshoe crab isn't a crustacean or a crab. It's an arthropod—a distant relative of the spider. In fact, tucked away beneath that shiny, hard shell, its body is surprisingly "spider-like." Yet, no spider was ever this odd! These strange sea creatures have ten eyes, five pairs of legs, and blue blood. Like starfish (class Asteroidea), they are able to regrow lost limbs. Their heart is in their head and their mouth is in their abdomen. With their tough armor, they have few enemies, apart from humans, who use them as fishing bait—which seems a sad use for such an incredible creature.

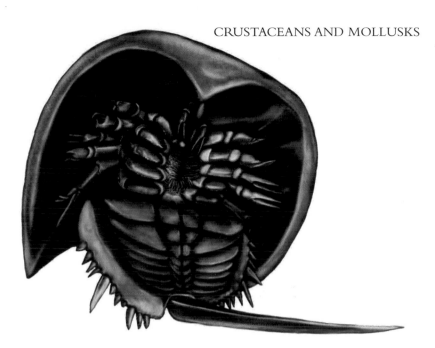

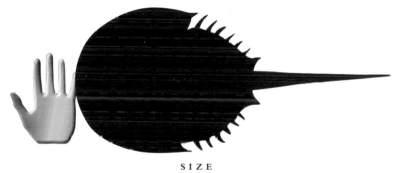

SIZE

Where in the world?

The Atlantic horseshoe (*Limulus polyphemus*) is a native of the Gulf of Mexico and the U.S. Atlantic coast. Other species are found in the Seto Inland Sea and Indian coastal waters.

MOST ANIMALS ON OUR PLANET have blood that contains hemoglobin. It's the hemoglobin that carries oxygen around the body. When it is exposed to air, the iron in hemoglobin oxidizes and the blood turns red. Horseshoe crab blood contains hemocyanin, which is copper-rich. The hemocyanin does the same job as hemoglobin, but because it is copper-based, it turns blue on contact with air.

Did you know?

● Horseshoe crabs are sometimes called living fossils because they resemble animals that have been found in fossils dating back 400 million years. However, *Limulus polyphemus* is a relatively recent arrival. It has been around for only about 20 million years—not long enough to earn the living fossil label.

● These armored beasts are regularly captured and "bled" because their blood is used in medical research.

● Horseshoe crabs have ten eyes located all over their bodies. Despite this, they have poor vision.

● That long pointed tail may look like a weapon, but it's really a lever. Horseshoe crabs move into the shallows to breed and often end up toppling over onto their backs. The tail helps them to right themselves.

Slipper Lobster

BODY
Decapod crustaceans have 19 body segments, which are divided between the head, thorax, and abdomen.

ABDOMEN
Six abdominal segments each bear a pair of pleopods for swimming and catching food.

THORAX
Three pairs of maxillipeds (mouthparts) and five pairs of walking legs are attached to the thorax.

HEAD & ANTENNAE
The head also holds a pair of broad, plate-like antennae, which have been adapted for digging.

HEAD & ANTENNULES
Five head segments contain mouthparts and a pair of stalk-like antennules, which explore the environment.

With a flattened body, truncated tail, and spade-like antennae, slipper lobsters look little like the true lobsters for which they are named. Although both groups have a similar, hard outer carapace, they're not closely related. The giveaway is that true lobsters have claws for trapping and dissecting prey—slipper lobsters don't. Instead, they rely on those broad antennae to dig around in the mud for crustaceans and other invertebrates. This strikingly colored group spends much of its time buried in sand on the sea bottom, emerging only at night to hunt. Luckily, they're not fussy eaters and will happily tuck into any corpse that they stumble across.

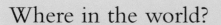

SIZE

Where in the world?

Slipper lobsters inhabit warm, shallow waters throughout the world's oceans. They are most often found sheltering in caves or muddy sea bottoms, or lurking amid thick beds of sea grass.

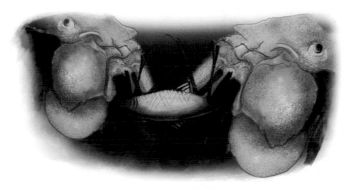

1. A FETID FISH ISN'T everyone's idea of a tasty snack, but these slipper lobsters aren't about to let good food go to waste. Scuttling over to the carcass, each eager crustacean tries to grab the free feast for itself. Neither lobster is prepared to share, so this lunchtime rush soon turns into a battle.

2. OUR COMBATANTS HAVE no offensive weapons to speak of, so they have to rely on persistence and pulling power. The determined decapods tug at the fish from either end until, eventually, the rotting flesh gives way, leaving one lobster the clear winner. The other lobster scuttles off, making do with the leftovers!

Did you know?

● Male and female slipper lobsters have no difficulty telling each other apart, but the only way for humans to spot who's who is by examining the lobster's legs! A pair of pincers on the fifth pair of walking legs shows that the lobster is a female.

● In French, these colorful crustaceans are called sea crickets because of the cricket-like noise they make under water.

● The tiny *Scyllarus pygmaeus* is the smallest known species of slipper lobster, growing to a maximum length of 2.2 in. (5.6 cm). The largest is *Scyllarides haanii*, which may reach up to 20 in. (50.8 cm) long.

● In Australia, slipper lobsters are often referred to as slipper bugs because, out of the water, they look like oversized beetles.

Cuttlefish

EYES
Cuttlefish can't see in color, but their eyes are among the most sophisticated in the animal world.

TENTACLES
Tentacles capture prey and take food to the mouth. They are lined with gripping suckers.

CHROMATOPHORES
Specialized cells in the skin enable the cuttlefish to make rapid changes to its coloration.

ARMS
In common with their cephalopod cousin, the squid, cuttlefish have eight arms plus two tentacles.

HEARTS
Two branchial hearts pump blood to the gills. A third pumps blood around the body.

These versatile invertebrates are real masters of disguise—able to change their appearance at will. With no internal skeleton, they can mold their bodies into all sorts of strange shapes and sizes. Their skin is packed with chromatophores, enabling them to change their color, too. This lets them camouflage themselves and also communicate with other members of their species. Like most cephalopods, they are intelligent and curious creatures, with a large brain-to-body ratio. The cuttlebone, for which they are named, is a gas-filled shell inside the mantle, which helps them regulate their buoyancy. These cuttlebones are fed to pet birds as calcium supplements!

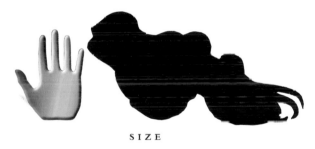

SIZE

CUTTLEFISH EYES ARE, STRUCTURALLY, VERY DIFFERENT from those of vertebrates. For instance, when vertebrates focus on an object, muscles change the shape of the lens in the eye. In cuttlefish, the whole shape of the eye is changed. Vertebrates also have a "blind spot," where the optic nerve passes through the retina. Cuttlefish have no blind spot because their optic nerve is positioned behind the retina.

Did you know?

● Most animals on our planet have blood that contains hemoglobin. It's the job of hemoglobin to carry oxygen around the body. The blood of most of the larger crustaceans, gastropods, and cephalopods contains hemocyanin instead of hemoglobin.

● Hemocyanin does the same job as hemoglobin, but it carries less oxygen. This means that cuttlefish blood has to circulate much more quickly to keep the cephalopod's body supplied with life-giving oxygen.

● Hemoglobin contains iron. When exposed to air, the iron oxidizes and the blood turns red.

● Hemocyanin is colorless, but as it is copper-based, it turns blue on contact with air. This makes many members of the mollusk and crustacean families real "blue bloods."

Where in the world?

Cuttlefish can be found around in coastal areas of all tropical and temperate oceans, except the Americas. Their preference is for shallow waters, especially sandy sea beds where they can hide.

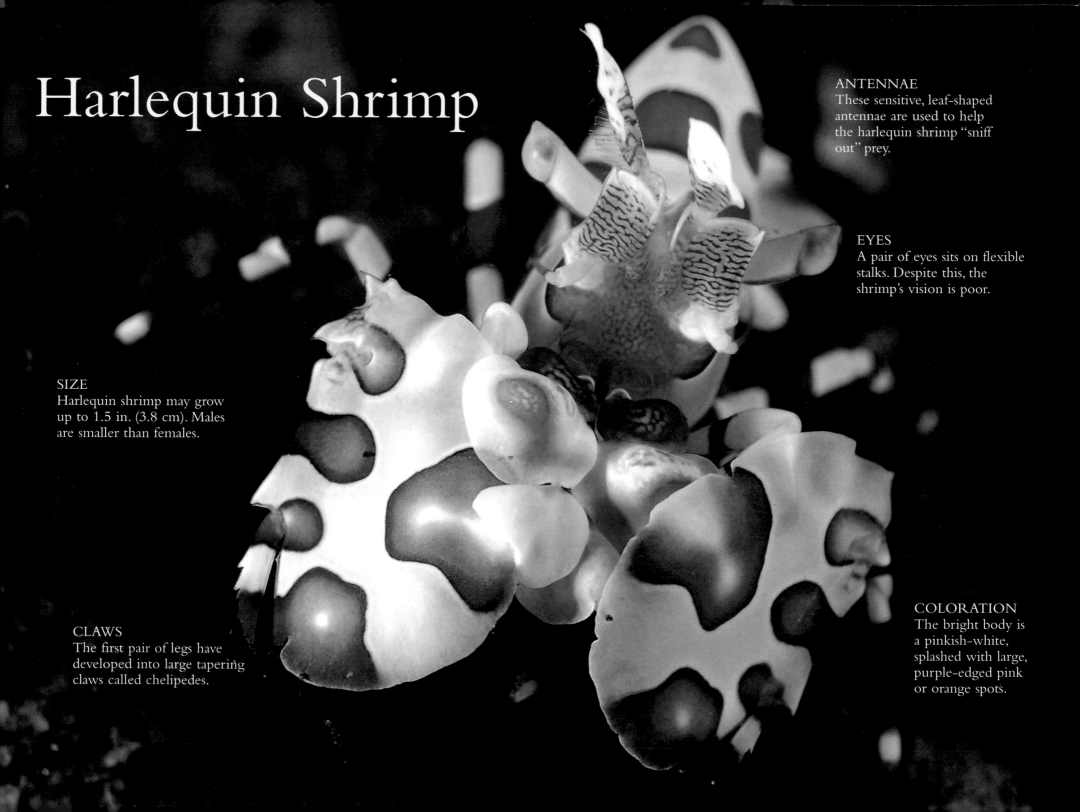

Harlequin Shrimp

ANTENNAE
These sensitive, leaf-shaped antennae are used to help the harlequin shrimp "sniff out" prey.

EYES
A pair of eyes sits on flexible stalks. Despite this, the shrimp's vision is poor.

SIZE
Harlequin shrimp may grow up to 1.5 in. (3.8 cm). Males are smaller than females.

CLAWS
The first pair of legs have developed into large tapering claws called chelipedes.

COLORATION
The bright body is a pinkish-white, splashed with large, purple-edged pink or orange spots.

Despite their colorful costume, little is known about the habits of these handsome harlequins. By day, they stay well hidden, using the bright colors of the coral reefs to blend in with their surroundings. At night, they come out to hunt. They're fussy eaters and prey only on starfish (class Asteroidea) and sea urchins (class Echinoidea). Such prickly prey present few problems for these accomplished hunters. There are even reports that some harlequins take advantage of the fact that starfish grow back lost limbs, to "farm" their captives. By tipping the echinoderm on its back so that it can't escape, they can eat one arm and return for another course, later, once the limb has regrown!

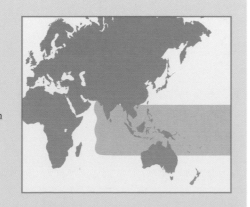

SIZE

Where in the world?

Harlequin shrimp are most at home in coral reefs and rocky coastlines in warm, tropical waters. These rare and beautiful creatures are found throughout the Indian and Pacific oceans.

1. HAULING ITS PREY BEHIND it, this harlequin looks like it's bitten off more than it can chew! These small shrimp eat only sea urchins and starfish, which have prickly shells and thick skin to protect them from predators. However, this hunter is not about to go hungry!

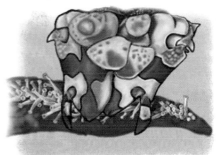

2. WITH THE HELP OF ITS MATE, it flips the starfish over on its back, exposing the soft flesh beneath. Now, it can eat. Its pincers may be small, but they are razor-sharp and, over the next few days, the harlequin slowly slices chunks of its still-living victim—beginning with the arms and working toward the soft body in the center.

Did you know?

● Harlequin shrimp come in a wide variety of colors, although they usually have pink, orange, or red spots. The abdominal legs of females have blue tips, while those of the males are white.

● Harlequins are named after a character from Italian opera who traditionally wears bright clothing. The harlequin is usually a comedian and an acrobat, who brings light relief to the play. However, he's based on a much darker character—the hellequin—who appears as an emissary of the Devil in medieval passion plays!

● These colorful crustaceans are also known as clowns, painted shrimp, and dancing shrimp.

● Harlequin couples stay together for life. After mating, the female lays between 100 and 5,000 eggs, which she devotedly tends and cleans until they hatch.

Index